WORLD WAR 2
US ARMY
FIGHTER
MODELING

OSPREY MASTERCLASS

WORLD WAR 2 US ARMY FIGHTER
MODELING

Jerry Scutts & Brett Green

OSPREY
PUBLISHING

First published in Great Britain in 2003 by
Osprey Publishing, Elms Court, Chapel Way,
Botley, Oxford OX2 9LP, United Kingdom.
Email: info@ospreypublishing.com

ISBN 1 84176 061 7

Editorial by Ilios Publishing, Oxford, UK
(www.iliospublishing.com)
Design: Ken Vail Graphic Design, Cambridge, UK
Index by David Worthington
Originated by Grasmere Digital Imaging, Leeds, UK
Printed in China through World Print Ltd.

03 04 05 06 07   10 9 8 7 6 5 4 3 2 1

A CIP catalog record for this book is available from the
British Library

FOR A CATALOG OF ALL BOOKS PUBLISHED BY
OSPREY MODELING, MILITARY AND AVIATION
PLEASE CONTACT:

Osprey Direct USA, c/o MBI Publishing, P.O. Box 1,
729 Prospect Ave, Osceola, WI 54020, USA
E-mail: info@ospreydirectusa.com

Osprey Direct UK, P.O. Box 140,
Wellingborough, Northants, NN8 2FA, UK
E-mail: info@ospreydirect.co.uk

www.ospreypublishing.com

CONTENTS

INTRODUCTION

Since beginning to collect plastic model airplane kits in the late 1950s/early 1960s, I realize looking back that I've witnessed the gradual growth of an entirely new hobby almost from day one. Little did I suspect what a thin-winged, blue plastic Airfix Spitfire packed into a polythene bag would lead to. It was not too long before there were enough models on the market for individuals to start to specialize in World War I aircraft, the RAF, the Luftwaffe or the USAAF and so on. The more models there were, the more this was possible – if only we'd had some decent references for the huge range of color schemes waiting to be unearthed. A full set of *Aircraft of the Fighting Powers* was only of limited help until William Green published *Famous Fighters of the Second World War* in 1961. That did it – we finally had a comprehensive overview of the main Allied and Axis fighters. Armed additionally with our monthly copies of *RAF Flying Review* and *Air Pictorial*, we began slowly to build up the picture although as far as we knew (or did not know) the data we had then was the very tip of the iceberg.

Color was virtually unknown in those days – the "real" equivalents of the gray shades seen in monochrome photographs were not even quoted, let alone published in color – but things did change with such milestone books as *Aircraft Camouflage and Markings 1907–1954*. This kept the pot boiling while Airfix (plus Frog, Revell, Aurora, etc.) continued to improve their kits. Special paints formulated for use on polystyrene plastic appeared and we began tentatively to finish models in the few alternative schemes we'd found in the references. The finished models probably weren't that good, but we enjoyed ourselves.

With regard to specialization, I simply can't remember when aircraft with stars and bars began to hold my interest – maybe it was when Airfix released their P-51D-5 of the 380th Fighter Squadron, 363d Fighter Group, named "Fool's Paradise IV." I doubt whether we'd even have been able to find those details then, but a silver aircraft finish was certainly a bit different to camouflage, so maybe that was it. In any event, that Airfix kit, plus a few others, more or less hooked me on the hobby of plastic modeling. As an idle mental exercise, I'm still wondering how long it took me to find the above data about that Mustang because few model companies then shared such with their customers.

Suffice to say that in trying to keep pace with the growth of an entire industry, albeit a small one by Wall Street standards, the supporting cast has often proved as fascinating as the stars. Many of us have, I suspect, had our interest in the various wartime air forces stimulated by a particularly good and new kit, and from this impetus other areas (dealing with the same subject) have beckoned, fed particularly by books and films. That more or less happened to me, the downside being that less and less time could realistically be devoted to simply building kits. I'm certainly not alone in confronting that dilemma.

These days, all I and numerous others can do is attempt to keep abreast of the flood of models and accessories, but some fundamental rules do not change: I trust therefore that the pages of this book inspire some to set aside a few hours a week to indulge themselves in what is after all a very absorbing pastime. At the time of writing, the references, the decals, the paints and the kits are on a different planet compared to the pioneering days, so much so that the subject of this book may be explored in great depth, at many different levels.

THE EARLY DAYS

The art of solid model airplane construction is now much easier than when the hobby first began to gain popularity during World War 2. Prior to then, making a model aircraft usually meant building it from a range of softwoods, balsa being the most popular. The complete airframe structure was usually built and then finally covered in tissue or other material. Little thought was given to the application of authentic markings, there being an almost total concentration on the aeronautical aspect and indeed, the desire to fly the finished model.

The availability of a number of kits containing pre-formed wooden parts and known initially as "solids" was a step forward for those who had no wish to actually fling their model into the air with the inherent risk of it being smashed beyond repair in the first heavy landing.

Those individuals would instead turn their hand to non-flying model kits, the range of which extended to many different types during World War 2. These reached a degree of sophistication and included pre-formed plastic propellers, canopy sections and wheels, but the skill level required to turn out a first rate model was still considerable.

Development of the industrial technique whereby polystyrene plastic could be injected into a metal mold to turn out pre-formed parts in great number, all of them exactly the same, was about to make a world of difference to one branch of the hobby of air-modeling. From large household items such as buckets and cups, the injection molding process made it possible to make a set of scaled components that, once assembled and glued together, constituted miniature airplanes and vehicles. No longer did the individual need to spend time whittling and forming the correct airfoil shape and fuselage contours out of wood, thus postponing the painting and finishing stages.

Plastic construction enabled a jump to be made to arguably the most interesting phase

of modeling, that of choosing a color scheme and applying it. Completion of a model airplane consequently became that much quicker and the emphasis changed completely from what might well be termed "structural" to "exterior." What went on under the skin was now of only passing interest to the model maker, who began searching for national insignia styles, camouflage patterns, code letters and personal markings applied to mark out a successful pilot.

Model kits of the early 1940s kept pace with aeronautical development, as while there was still some emphasis on the airplanes of World War 1, those of the then current conflict soon became the core subject for the manufacturers. Allied and Axis types predominated while American fighters were understandably few: the prototypes of the famous fighters of World War 2 were only then being tested but to provide an international balance, kits were released of such exotica as the Curtiss YP-37. A popular one, it remained available for some time as the P-37. How many kits of the early Curtiss fighter do we have today?

ABOVE Tamiya's recent 1/48-scale P-47D Thunderbolt is beautifully detailed, accurate and provides plenty of options for the modeler. This kit represents the current standard in a hobby that has been developing for half a century.

North American
MUSTANG III
Ready to Assemble Plastic Model of the Famous World War II Fighter!

1/32 Scale

Revell

FUSELAGE 12"
WINGSPAN 14"

ABOVE Revell's 1/32-scale kits of the 1960s were highly desirable models in their day. Many of these kits featured operating control surfaces, retracting landing gear and sliding canopies. Unfortunately, due to the requirement for styrene hinges and rails, these working features often robbed the model of finesse and impacted on accuracy. Kits of the 1960s frequently sported thousands of oversized rivets. Revell's 1/32-scale P-51B/Mustang III kits certainly fell into this category! However, a few kits from this era are still worth building today.

EARLY MARKINGS

Along with the components themselves, manufacturers of the early plastic kits included a set of markings to cover the basic essentials of national insignia and so forth, so that when they appeared in due course, a reasonable looking example of the P-51, P-47 or P-38 could be built. In some model releases, their designers were so demonstrably worried that the simple task of applying national insignia via waterslide decals (transfers) might be misinterpreted that they scribed the outlines into the surface. Fortunately, this practice did not last very long.

Early model airplane kit transfer sheets made few concessions to authentic markings such as code letters or ID numbers and those that were included were seemingly chosen at random. Sheets of checkers and numbers became available, these being little more than recognition aids based on flying model decoration. And kits of wartime fighters made in America usually had USAF rather than USAAF national insignia – so again, it is not hard to see how far we've come in this respect alone.

WHICH SCALE?

The outline accuracy of these early construction kits was not always all it might have been and the question of scale – i.e. one model comparable

with another in terms of relative dimensions – was sometimes even dictated by the size of the box the model came in. This made for some very odd "between scale" parts, often too small to take full advantage of the subject. This was true of larger aircraft such as bombers however, the fighters being a generally more convenient size with which to work.

Once there was a perceived market, the industry in the United States soon became organized and manufacturers released most plastic models in what is sometimes referred to as "quarter scale." This translated the full-size aircraft's dimensions to model components that measured out at a quarter of an inch to the foot. This scaling could be entirely relied upon, as non-conformist models continued to appear, but in general bigger was better in the US. Interestingly, the UK market had already appreciated the undoubted advantages of models in this larger scale. The Chingford Model Aerodrome (CMA) was, by 1944, offering a range of quarter-scale solid models which included a P-38, P-39 and P-47.

Equally popular was the 1/72-scale range by Truscale of Bournemouth, UK, which as early as 1940 had released an Airacobra and Tomahawk. At that time of course the US Air Corps had few other full-size designs of which models could be made. That did not mean American fighters were overlooked and lacking anything more developed for service use: the P-37 had to suffice until details were released of the Bell YP-63 and the early P-40s. Dimensionally about half the size of a 1/48-scale model in terms of a single-seat fighter, each of these smaller kits included pre-formed wings and fuselage, metal propellers, hardwood cowlings, national insignia transfers and glue. Again there was a lack of squadron markings, probably due to wartime national security restrictions.

With the war over there was a temporary revision to traditional model aircraft pending reorganization of the industry from wartime to peacetime footing. When plastic kits became available in England, there was a general swing towards 1/72 scale, while the Americans generally stayed loyal to the larger scale. Those kits that crossed the Atlantic from the US always carried the penalty of a higher price, and in "pocket money" terms, the low price of a bagged Airfix kit successfully created a firm brand loyalty – despite their relative crudity compared to what came later. Another reason was that these kits successfully tapped into the "collector" instinct, for Airfix, Frog and other

manufacturers put out a steadily increasing number of subjects. With regard to single-seat fighters, although the finished results were quite small they were convenient to build and easy to line up along a bedroom shelf. Additions to the smaller scale soon overtook the fewer 1/48-scale models that appeared in those days simply because there were fewer of the latter and they were not always easy to obtain.

As time passed and the product generally improved, model company engravers became increasingly aware that the necessary heavy metal molds for plastic kits were adaptable and capable of reproducing components with very fine scale detail. On the actual plastic the work of toolmakers appeared as raised or recessed panels, lines of rivets and numerous optional parts designed to enable the builder to complete one or more versions of the same aircraft.

Models of the machines that flew in the colors of the United States Army Air Forces were early arrivals on the plastic modeling scene and the popularity of the "big three" (the P-51 Mustang, P-47 Thunderbolt and P-38 Lightning) was quickly established. That

LEFT Old books can sometimes be found at bargain prices. Many books from earlier decades are still valuable reference sources. All of the books pictured here were published in the 1960s. They feature a wealth of wartime photos, and these images are as relevant today as they were when they were first published. However, be aware that research has uncovered new facts about aircraft variants, details and color schemes over the years, so color profiles and drawings in these old books may need verification against modern sources.

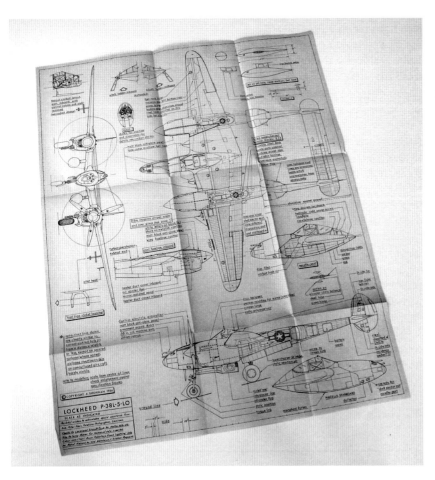

As the war progressed, basic markings schemes for American fighters developed to encompass local conditions, the various configurations of the aircraft and above all, the need for concealment on the ground and instant recognition in the air. Each theater of war had its own detail requirements for markings although there was a considerable degree of commonality regarding paintwork, once the early-war anomalies resulting from diverted contracts settled into standardization.

These often conflicting requirements of blending into the terrain to elude the enemy and being recognized by pilots on the same side resulted in a plethora of colors, code letters, numbers, bands and stripes being applied to all US fighters in combat. Reliable and adaptable systems soon emerged.

EUROPEAN BASIS

Arguably the most effective markings system used on US fighters during World War 2 was developed for the RAF whereby each unit was given a code consisting of two letters (sometimes a letter and a number) with a third letter identifying the individual "plane-in-squadron." There was far less visual confusion after this system was adopted, but the first American fighters based in England were also given an additional recognition scheme. Thus white nose, wing and tail bands over camouflage finish marked out the P-47 and P-51, fighters that could conceivably be confused with their common German adversaries, the Fw 190 and Bf 109 respectively. Untold numbers of Thunderbolt and Mustang pilots probably owe their lives to this paint scheme as they dived through bomber formations in pursuit of the Luftwaffe Jagdflieger. "Friendly fire" incidents continued to occur but the white bands minimized this risk.

Colors were used as an additional recognition aid and so diverse did these become that the whole subject of aircraft markings eventually became a separate field of study, largely divorced from technical development, combat operations and first-hand pilot narratives. Many of those wartime fighter color schemes, matching a well-documented key, survived via an unprecedented visual and written record, so that 60 years on the publication of still photographs and the widespread availability of movie film footage enable the enthusiast model maker to acquire a comprehensive library of reference.

Books devoted entirely to the subject of wartime American fighters are legion, be it their technical development, performance, the

this popularity has hardly ever waned is not difficult to explain. So many of the decisive air combats of the war were fought by American and Allied pilots flying these types and, via their fathers, youngsters were imbued with a keen sense of patriotism.

FIGHTER VERSATILITY

With ten air forces in the field by 1944, all of them with their fighter component, the USAAF had, like most air arms of the fighting powers, come to appreciate the effectiveness and economy of pursuit aircraft, those the pilots first nicknamed "pea shooters." The role of a category of aircraft historically regarded in the US as much less useful than bombers had changed radically. Very early on in World War 2, American fighters were adapted – and soon built – to carry external ordnance, which brought their basic combat duty partially into the realm of the bomber. Burgeoning numbers of single- and multi-seater fighter bombers now demanded a comprehensive system of markings schemes aimed at rapid air-to-air and "friend from foe" recognition. Different theaters of war saw different fighter markings schemes, for instance those of Europe and the Pacific regions.

combat record of their pilots, or the camouflage and markings the aircraft carried. With this gradual increase in quantity and quality of printed material, the model manufacturers were made aware of what people wanted to build as three-dimensional replicas; for their part the makers had to gamble that the enormous financial investment in metal molds and indeed the plastic raw material would be justified by high volume sales.

As polystyrene plastic is a by-product of oil, its cost is volatile. There have been periods when supplies of "black gold" indirectly curtailed the production of new kit releases, or forced prices up. But in the main the output has more than kept pace with demand at generally reasonable cost. In time, the scale accuracy of successive releases improved to the point where today, individual kits are about as true to the original machine as anyone is likely to get. In a competitive world, plastic kit manufacturers will of course duplicate some items, particularly the better-known wartime US fighters. "If it sells, it should be in our range," is the understandable view inside the industry.

This fact has also driven the search for definitive quality, something that has only benefited the modeler. These days, scales that were previously neglected have also had new items regularly added so that with a few notable exceptions, a range of US fighters can be built in all five popular scales from 1/100 to 1/24. Not quite so popular, simply because the number of kits is so small (and the investment by the supplier so large), is 1/24 scale.

The smallest of the scales has had some real gems added to it over the years and many people find the tiny single-engine fighters that result just right for them. One advantage here is if the modeler wishes to portray a scene that includes multiple aircraft. A whole group of Mustangs or Thunderbolts, even a factory production line for example, would suit 1/100 (or 1/144) scale subjects very well without the need to own the equivalent of a full-size hanger in which to store the finished articles.

EXPANDING THE POSSIBILITIES

In parallel with the increase in the number and diversity of injection-molded construction kits, the more limited runs possible with the vacuum-formed (vacuform) plastic process has enabled even more gaps, represented by the more obscure types or variants, to be filled. This means that if the modeler desires, say, a P-39 in 1/32 scale, it is possible to build one, provided that the undeniable extra work stages demanded by this type of kit are taken into account.

The range of kit options has been further boosted by the rise of companies specializing in conversion sets, usually of particular items – wheels, radomes, fairings, flaps and so forth – designed to be incorporated into injection molded kit parts to enable an alternative earlier or later production variant to be produced. In many cases, these conversion sets offer more accurate replacement parts because the specialist is seemingly able to focus more closely on a particular area of an aircraft replica than the commercial supplier is.

BELOW The development of the hobby over the past decades allows us now to produce authentic miniature replicas of our favorite aircraft.

CHAPTER 1
GETTING STARTED

BELOW LEFT Different adhesives are available for different requirements. Cyanoacrylate cement, more commonly known as superglue, is helpful for securing small parts. This glue dries very quickly, but the bond is somewhat brittle and the fumes from the drying glue can fog clear parts. Watchmakers' cement is a good alternative for bonding clear parts. It is strong and clear when dry. There are many choices of cement for gluing polystyrene plastic parts. The Revell "Contacta" cement pictured is equipped with a handy needle applicator for precise placement of the cement.

BELOW RIGHT Sanding tools are an essential element of the modeling toolbox. From the left, we can see a sanding stick, a buffing stick and emery board. These can all be cheaply obtained from the supermarket or pharmacy. The needle file permits smoothing of hard-to-reach areas of your model, and the sanding block is ideal when large areas of plastic need to be re-contoured.

Getting started on a modern kit is therefore easy and requires very little extra financial outlay over and above a set of paints and a few basic tools. The latter will vary according to the individual's taste but the successful completion of any kit requires a set number of steps to be followed before any gluing of parts is undertaken. These include immersing the entire set of carrier sprues in a solution of washing up liquid in lukewarm water. This is necessary to remove any traces of the "release agent" used, as the term implies, to slip each sprue out of the mold smoothly, with no pulling or sticking and without a film of thin plastic known as "flash" inadvertently embracing the component parts. This very thin plastic film still appears on some modern kits but in general it has been eliminated from the products of the major manufacturers, whose quality control is generally of a high order. A thin film of plastic has its uses in some areas of modeling as it is strong enough to shape into extra panels, to replicate into battle damage areas and so forth – so follow the old adage of "never throw anything away." Even the carrier sprues have their uses. Stretched under a flame those long straight sections of plastic have historically been the source of ultra thin aerial wires on innumerable models. The advantage is of course that, being plastic rather than any other material, you can rely on its strength and ability to bond as well as the kit components.

In my experience though you need to experiment with the plastic used by various manufacturers. As will be noticed when assembling the kit, some plastics have a softer compound than others. The ability to "string" the heated sprues to thin lengths depends on the degree of density.

When each washed sprue has dried, some of the parts need to be removed from the carrier frame, a task that always requires great care, particularly where small, delicate components are concerned. These should not be pulled or twisted away from the sprue as a pit may easily be made in the smooth surface of the component which will require filing off or, in extreme cases, filling and sanding down. Some kits are better than others in this respect: occasionally it seems that no matter how careful you are at separating the parts from the sprues, a tiny raised area remains on the component and stubbornly refuses to disappear. It is therefore an area that always needs close attention and a "damage limitation" approach right from the start. This applies particularly to the canopy and other transparent parts. Plastic kits have historically been packed into polythene bags – several bags in the case of some larger scale models – and I always take the precaution against transparencies getting scratched by leaving them in one of the bags. Alternatively, wrap them in tissue paper. Don't let the clear parts rattle around in the box because they are prone to damage and breakage in extreme cases.

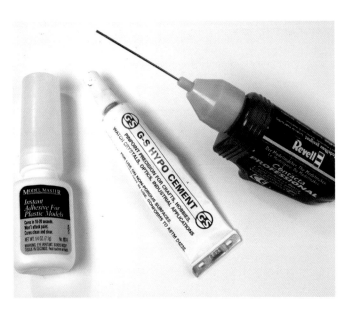

TOP LEFT Here are three, different-sized hobby knives and two pairs of scissors. These will be some of your most frequently used modeling tools.

TOP RIGHT A high quality sprue cutter (on the left of this picture) will supply a clean cut and save a great deal of time that might otherwise be spent trimming, sanding and filling. A selection of razor saws will also find their way into the modeling toolbox.

MIDDLE LEFT Different tools are required for different uses. Each of these tools (pliers, tweezers and a self-closing hemostat) has a particular application.

MIDDLE RIGHT Here are some tools that change the surface texture of a model. two different styles of scriber and a dressmaker's pin wheel. The latter is an inexpensive tool useful for replicating rivet marks in plastic.

BOTTOM LEFT A pin vise is simply a small drill that holds tiny drill bits. This is another frequently used element of the tool kit.

BOTTOM RIGHT It will usually be necessary to fill scams or gaps on a model. A large selection of putties is available for this purpose. The old letter opener at the top of the picture is used as a trowel for applying and smoothing putty.

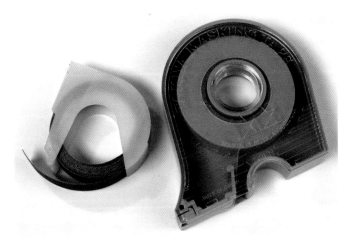

ABOVE LEFT Tape is useful in many aspects of modeling. The Dymo tape on the left can be used as a self-adhesive scribing guide on large kit parts, while Tamiya Masking Tape can be used for preparing kits for painting.

ABOVE RIGHT No modeling toolkit would be complete without a selection of good quality paintbrushes in various sizes. An airbrush is an important tool to help achieve a realistic finish. The airbrush pictured here is Testor's Aztek A470.

TOOLS

In recommending the tools needed to get a kit project underway, the separation of parts from the sprue will require a strong pair of tin snips or sprue cutters to sever the often tough "trees" that hold the pieces in position. These attachments have to be fairly substantial, as some kits need to be shipped halfway around the world before they reach the modeler's hands. Stacked on shelves, not always by people who appreciate the delicacy of what's inside, they can get damaged; so strong retaining pins are needed on each of the sprue frames. Tin snips will easily remove the most important parts including the two fuselage halves, the engine cowling and the wing sections in order for the modeler to make the initial dry or "dummy run." Carefully check the fit of all these components, ensuring especially that the attachment pins align correctly. If they don't, an unsightly seam or step might result when the glue is applied which will laboriously have to be sanded down. If pin alignment threatens to create this fault, trim off any offending ones at this stage. Other useful tools are dealt with in the images and captions on pages 12–14.

BUILDING A P-47

Our "getting started" modeling subject will be the P-47 Thunderbolt, with particular reference to Tamiya's 1/48-scale P-47D Thunderbolt "Razorback", modeled by Brett Green in the images that accompany this chapter.

With such a variety of P-47 kits available, across several scales, it's always a good idea to check the wing and fuselage sections for outline accuracy against a multi-view drawing. Plans of P-47s showing three or more views of the aircraft have been published in magazines and books in great number and few modelers will be unaware that they vary a good deal and that the most modern plans are not necessarily the most reliable. The answer is to use the one you feel best represents the full size machine in order to check the dimensions of plastic kit parts against what is, after all, a "flat" and therefore false representation – and indeed one that no manufacturer ever needs to build the real aircraft.

I take the view that scale plans are only part of the literature the modeler needs on World War 2 aircraft and nobody should rely one hundred percent on their accuracy. After all, a plan is only another individual's interpretation of a three dimensional object in one plane – which of course has been drawn up, reduced in size and reproduced, a process with numerous opportunities for error.

A friend who draws scale plans for side views has made good use of a computer to measure dimensions between known points on an airframe and come up with some surprising answers. But those of us who are not professional draughtsmen or engineers may not fully understand the close tolerances aerodynamists have to work with – nor do we really need to know for the purposes of modeling. My overall advice is to run your eye over what you consider to be the most reliable plans but make a close concurrent study of the best possible quality photographs.

Read any model magazine and sooner or later there will be some pundit who will inform the listening world that such and such a manufacturer's kit is two millimeters too short in the fuselage. Really? What if the plan used was scaled down from an original drawing (as most reproduced plans are) and happened to be undersized by just that amount? How would our "expert" know that?

Dimensions can of course be checked with a scale rule or calculator – provided that the reference that quotes the figure seems right.

Fine – but now check another book, then a third or fourth. Chances are that someone will have added a few eighths of an inch to the quoted overall length. My personal view is simply to ignore any tiny discrepancy between kit and plan that is not glaringly obvious or that does not exceed about five millimeters. It seems that few people can ever get these questions of dimensions totally right, for the above reasons which are often beyond one's control. I feel that it is simply not worth the effort involved to add some tiny extension to a kit, one probably involving a good deal of work, that few observers will even notice unless it is brought to their attention. Obviously shape matters and if an error in the overall length of the P-47's fuselage is a result of a poorly defined rudder or a short nose, then some remedial work should be undertaken.

As your modeling experience builds, so will your "third eye" improve. This hypothetical combination of gray matter and optics is an aid to accuracy in reproduction and will come into play a great deal in modeling good scale replica of aircraft. Study of photographs will also reveal the finer points of design and construction of the full-size machine, those "make or break" areas that have to be spot-on for a model to work in its own right. Sooner or later the common pitfall areas, those where the kit manufacturer has to pay close attention to

his own plans in order to produce an accurate replica, will be quickly noticed and closely checked before anything else.

COMMON PROBLEM AREAS FOR MODELERS

All machines have their idiosyncrasies of design, none more than aircraft so it seems. On the Thunderbolt there are a number of areas that can be problematic if they have been poorly designed as kit components or if there has been some fault in the moldings. If the P-47 kit version is a "razorback" model prior to the P-47D-25, the top line and shape of the rear fuselage will stand out if it clearly lacks the true sharpness obvious in a three-quarter-rear view of the full-size aircraft. If you feel that the Thunderbolt looks better with the canopy open, try positioning the kit cockpit before cutting it from the windscreen. Chances are that it won't fit, and will ride a scale foot or so too high. The reason for this disparity is that the greenhouse canopy on pre-D-25 versions of the Thunderbolt was very thin. Two handles set into the lower framing were used by the pilot to brace the canopy apart so that it would align in the runners on each side of the fuselage. It had to be thin to be light enough to move easily and align snugly with the coaming behind the pilot's seat. Therefore, scaling it all

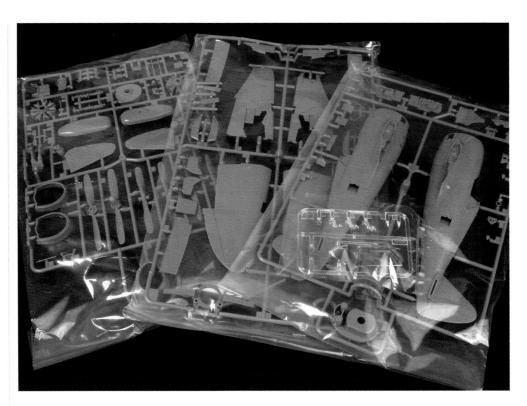

RIGHT The sprues of Tamiya's 1/48-scale P-47D Thunderbolt are packed in separate plastic bags. This is important, as it prevents parts on different sprues from rubbing together while the box is in transit, which could result in fine scratches and scuffing. The sprues contain a wealth of options for the kit, including bombs, rocket launchers, different styles of drop tanks, alternate propellers and optional position landing flaps, cowl flaps and fuselage outlet.

down means that no razorback model fuselage section is really going to be narrow enough if the clear section is to align with it when open.

Depending on the desired scale, the modeler has to chose either to fit a canopy from another kit that is slightly oversized (they all vary to some degree) or mold one in material thin enough to sit far enough down to rest on the sliding rail and generally line up squarely when located in the open position. The only other option is to laboriously pare down the plastic behind the cockpit until it will accept the clear section that is supplied with the kit.

The chord and shape of the rudder has also presented a few challenges to Thunderbolt kits in the past, as have areas such as the alignment of the eight blast tubes of the wing machine guns, the overall shape of the cowling, the size

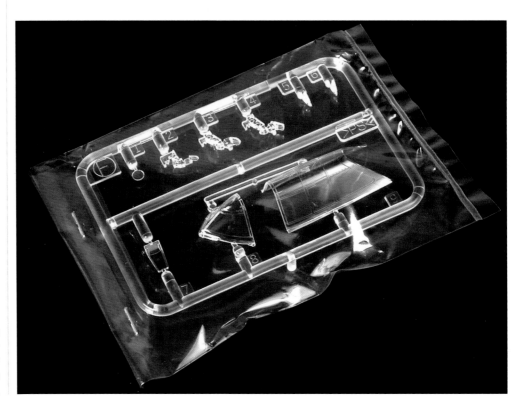

RIGHT It is even more important that the clear parts are packed separately as they are far more susceptible to scratching.

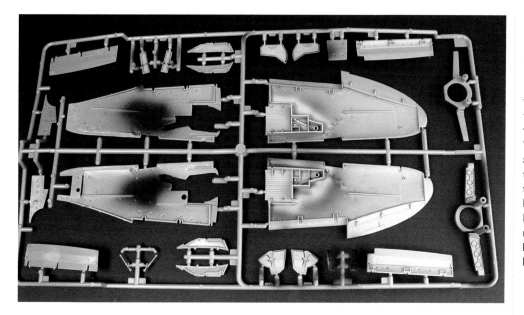

and shape of the fuselage turbo waste gates, the cowl flaps and the canopy.

Taking these check points in no particular order, the chord and outline shape of the rudder should be checked against photos and plans. As is well known, all eight machine guns should be set in a horizontal line and not follow the dihedral angle of the wing; the turbo should be well defined, with the two small exhaust doors aft of the cowling sitting proud of the fuselage; all cowl flaps should also be thin enough for the scale and preferably not all in a "wide-open" position, and the large ventral exhaust ports should be the correct size and shape.

A common scale problem on Thunderbolt kits is that the waste gates for the turbocharger on each side of the center fuselage are often too thick if the moveable doors are molded open. Even if they come as separate items they should be to scale thickness.

You'll also need to check whether or not the main landing gear doors are in their correct three sections. On older kits, they might well be molded as one piece that has to be cut into three. That tiny door section at the top of each oleo leg seems to throw manufacturers, who often mold it as a protuberance at the top of the "straight" section of the doors. In extreme cases I've known kits to ignore these tiny doors completely and merely engrave their outline on the outside face of the main door. Although these items are very small, without them the P-47's unusual extending oleo would have been exposed to more dust and grit   and once you know the doors should be separate sections, your conscience will create a need to reproduce them.

As with all World War 2 fighters, the forward rake of the undercarriage and the toe-in of the wheels of the P-47 need careful attention: certain kits are seemingly designed to make this alignment more difficult to achieve but if you feel they have it wrong, modify the locating pins – or do your own thing!

Other areas of P-47 kits that need scrutiny include the shell case exit doors in the wing undersides, how well the detail of the attached (or separate) main wing racks for drop tanks and bombs has been achieved, and of course, the outline shape of the cockpit canopy, not forgetting the unique shape of the windscreen on the early model razorbacks.

Aircraft details can look remarkably different from certain camera angles, and with the P-47 the upper line of the forward fuselage will appear to vary considerably. This optical illusion has led kit manufacturers something of a dance insofar as designing the best way to attach the cowling to the fuselage and "mold the dip" that always appeared where the fuselage curved downwards to meet the cowl flaps. The way the flaps are molded in the kit often has a bearing on accuracy of outline. Various approaches have been adopted by kit manufacturers to attach the cowling and the engine components, but they usually comprise a straight join involving cementing the circumference of the cowling.

Underneath, the Thunderbolt (depending on the sub-type) can appear different as well – quite pot-bellied in some views and regularly curved in others. Some machines from the P-47C-5 did indeed have an extra "keel" section to enable strengthened belly tank/bomb shackles to be fitted. There was a distinct bulge on the underside as a result. But the trouble with that kind of modification is that it raises the following question: were all sub-types similar in outline from that point on? If the

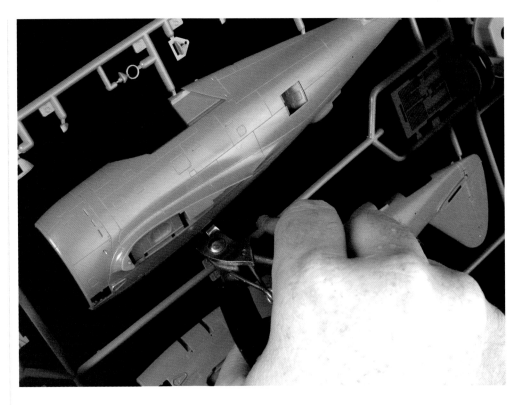

RIGHT Next, major parts are removed from the kit sprues using sprue cutters. These can be used to make a clean cut close to the plastic part, minimizing later "clean-up."

answer is a qualified no, it does not actually help the modeler much. Comparing the kit parts to as many photos as possible is the only way to decide if the plastic matches the metal.

CONSTRUCTION TIME

So, having washed all the parts on the sprues and thoroughly scrutinized what came out of the box, and assuming that the P-47 kit you are building is accurate enough not to require major surgery with a file or scalpel, construction of the main sub-assemblies can proceed. By this stage you will have cut off the two fuselage halves and the wing to see how they match up.

It goes without saying that you also need to check that the horizontal tailplanes are ready for assembly the right way up. This is because they may have previously been detached and sub-assembled. In case you have done this preparatory work but neglected to check if the trim tabs and any prominent mass balances are where they should be, consult the instructions, which should make this clear. The same goes for trim tabs on the ailerons and the wings. I've seen numerous references to the fact that kit manufacturers have left these on the kit when they were in fact omitted from a given sub-type. And of course the opposite is also true, so knowledge of the sub-type of aircraft you're working with is quite important. These are annoying details to find out later when painting a trim tab that your particular variant did not in fact have!

THE CUTTING EDGE

Previous mention of a scalpel brings us to another essential item in our tool kit. Any form of sharp knife will suffice to cut what is usually relatively soft plastic, including those that have snap-off blades. Those by Swann Morton, sold with a range of different-shaped blades, are probably the most versatile. I find a 10A blade to be the most useful for trimming plastic components, as it is not too long to risk breakage. Also, the blade remains sharp enough to enable repeated trimming or scraping lightly along a seam to remove a glue bubble without any surface scratching, as happens when using the "wet and dry" sanding method. Those annoying hairline seams that can appear on upper and lower wing surfaces when gluing – no how matter how careful you've been during the dry runs – can easily be removed by a scalpel held at an angle to the offending joint.

Also, I invariably use Swann Morton blades as drills. Gently rotated, the pointed blades are ideal for making that extra locating hole or opening out a gun trough. Provided that due restraint is exercised (the blades otherwise being liable to snap in half or at least lose their tip) such work can be completed without resort to an electric drill. Patience, that supreme modeling aid, applies. A round file can be used to clean up the machine-gun port, intake or whatever area you need to drill out. On P-47s a wing root camera port may need to be added if the kit does not indicate it.

"Wet and dry" sandpaper is usually sold in sheets varying in surface roughness, with the working side in black with a plain backing. It is one of those time-tested modeling aids that is invaluable for a whole range of sanding from very light to heavy duty. Repeat usage will result in a very smooth surface that remains ideal for very light sanding of canopy edges and so forth. Any heavy sanding is best carried out with a sheet of wet and dry attached to a firm base and onto which considerable pressure may be applied.

If scratches on the plastic surface persist despite liberal use of wet and dry, a proprietary metal polish product such as Duraglit Silvo will add that final sheen. The subsequent coat(s) of paint should cover the surface abrasions, particularly when applied by airbrush. Care needs to be taken when using any abrasive however worn it might be as there is a risk of removing the paint under that authentic sheen you're trying to achieve. Scratches on canopy sections are particularly annoying but polishing with ordinary toothpaste can restore clarity.

FILLERS

In extreme cases, where a coat or two of paint will clearly not cover gaps or surface abrasions, model filler or what is generally termed "body putty" should be used. My personal choice is Green Putty, an American product that has been on the market for many years but has since been joined by similar products produced elsewhere. Even the best-fitting kits may require a tiny spot of putty, particularly if the mold maker has been a little over enthusiastic with extracting component parts from the locating pins inside the mold. This action sometimes leaves a sink mark or dimple or two on the plastic surface, which should be filled. Never use too much, as the rubbing down process may itself create supplementary indentations, which also need filling! All such putties intended for use with polystyrene plastic are pliable as they come out of the tube and remain so for as long as they need to be induced into gaps. Left to harden off overnight, they can then be smoothed off to the point where any unsightly join line is all but invisible.

Having gone through the above initial stages, the modeler should have all the main sub assemblies trimmed and ready for sticking together and the fuselage sections cleaned up ready for mating. Don't forget to lightly roughen the butt joint edges to improve adhesion. Then comes the question of painting the interior of the Thunderbolt's cockpit.

Fortunately the P-47 had quite a crowded crew position and with the seat, armor plate, instrument panel, gun sight and control column *in situ*, few of the details on the fuselage sidewalls can readily be seen, due mainly to the curvature of the fuselage at that point. This means that a black "shadow coat" followed by base coat of Dull Dark Green, with some structural parts painted in zinc chromate and black can be all that is needed.

VARIED SHADES

There were several shades of protective chromate paint used on USAAF aircraft, most of them varying from yellow to a liverish green. These days most model paint manufacturers include a chromate green as part of their range and the shade chosen will be one of the first

ABOVE The P-47D propeller assembly is broken down in a unique fashion that accurately represents the join between the front and rear of the hub, and also guarantees the correct pitch for the propeller blades. This little assembly was prepared by painting the hub silver, followed by a wash of black oil paint to highlight bolt detail. The propeller blades were then painted black with yellow tips.

LEFT The P-47D engine comprises only eight parts but the detail is very good indeed Careful detail painting and an oil wash maximized the detail on the plastic parts.

paints to be applied to the model. Areas such as the tailwheel and mainwheel wells and the edges of the undercarriage doors which on P-47s, were often quite visible as a chrome yellow/orange shade, need to be so treated.

Some P-47 kits extend to a canvas dust boot around the tailwheel oleo and this may need to be painted at this stage, along with the two retaining rods that keep the tailwheel doors open. Simulated on some kits, these rods may be added as separate items if the modeler so wishes. The cockpit console and sidewalls also need painting at this stage, as do the seat and all areas of the cockpit visible through the canopy.

Most fighter models require the cockpit detail to be completed at an early stage, as this sub-assembly will be trapped by the fuselage halves when they are glued. Some items such as a separate headrest and radio sets that are located aft of the pilot's seat may be left until later. As a considerable degree of handling of the model lies ahead, you don't need flimsy parts that are liable to come lose snapping off and perhaps being lost forever.

To sum up, the less you really need to add before the aircraft has its fuselage and perhaps wings assembled, the better.

WORTH A THOUSAND WORDS?

By studying the accompanying instruction sheet, the modeler will now have a good idea of how the kit has been broken down for ease of assembly and the number of stages this will take.

I find that kit instructions always need a modicum of personal interpretation at certain stages of construction although familiarity with the aircraft type will soon enable much of the assembly to be completed without constant reference to them. In recent years manufacturers have almost dispensed with the cost of translating instructions into six-plus languages and instead have reverted to illustrations. This means that anyone from Yorktown to Yokahama is theoretically able to assemble the kit with the minimum of trouble – certainly not because a word (or ten) cannot be understood. In fact kit design for American single-engine fighter models follows much the same pattern and few people should run into difficulties in assembling a Thunderbolt. On the other hand, the various stages have to be clearly understood to ensure that the sheet does not suggest, for example, that the assembly of the main landing gear is not tackled too early. It is well known that alignment of a kit's wings and tailplane against the vertical is vital: if the dihedral angle is too steep, the landing gear oleos will invariably be too high and the wheel toe-in (or out) will suffer. Vertical alignment of the mainwheels also needs to be carefully done, so the landing gear assembly should ideally to be completed at the same time.

Should the kit instructions suggest early attachment of the gear, ignore them. Applying adhesive to all three undercarriage legs must wait until the wing angle has been obtained satisfactorily, otherwise even the best model risks gaining a few scale degrees of dihedral on

RIGHT The Tamiya kit's instrument panel is quite good. It features blank instruments and offers the option of either painting the dials or applying a decal over the top of the whole panel. Instead, I decided to apply individual instrument decals for each of the dials after punching them from Tamiya's kit decal sheet. A Waldron micro Punch and Die was used for this precision task.

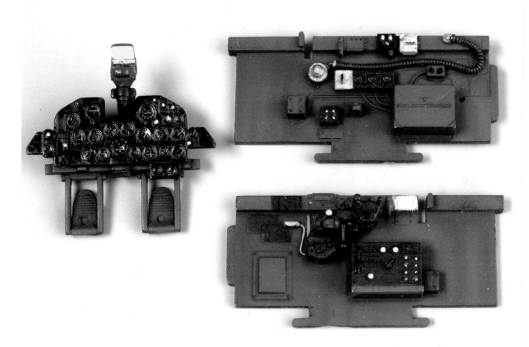

LEFT The individual decals were sealed with a spot of floor wax to reinforce the impression of a glass lens in front of each instrument. The detail on the Tamiya P-47D kit's sidewalls looks great too. Detail in silver, white, red and even semi-gloss black (over the flat black base coat) was picked out with a fine paintbrush.

one wing compared with the opposite side while the adhesive that fixes them in position dries out. Unsightly gaps may also appear at the wing roots and require use of filler and sandpaper to eliminate them. But if basic precautions are taken, the dry-run fitting of parts should result in a near perfect marrying up all round.

Wing to fuselage joints often pose problems in alignment, as do other major components that are molded separately to one another on the sprue. There can be few things more irksome than to have a wing jut forward of the root fillet section and overhang at the trailing edge. What to do? In extreme cases the only remedy is to employ filler to build up the fillet before the wing halves are joined to it. Then, using ample adhesive, aim to obtain as firm a bond as possible before sanding the offending joint down after the wing is attached. How much work you'll have to do depends on the design of the kit in question, but the butt joint is still commonly used on models of P-47s and single-engine aircraft of similar configuration.

ADDING MORE DETAIL

Should you now be a little impatient to complete your Thunderbolt and add the finishing touches, there is no reason why time need be spent on adding extra detail to the cockpit area. Today most good kits, including the excellent Tamiya one shown in the photographs that accompany this chapter, come with all that the modeler needs to give the required depth to this area, including decals to be attached to a plastic section representing the instrument panel. Cockpit sidewalls, with their various instruments, boxes and levers, are invariably molded in relief and need only careful painting and maybe a little additional dry brush wear and tear, to bring them out. Paint the inside as accurately as possible, both from your references and the kit instructions.

It is of course entirely an individual choice how much additional work to put into the cockpit interior. For example, do you want merely to pick out the seat harness with paint, or add your own from a multi-media accessory kit, such as the Eduard one shown in the photograph on page 22? Having decided whether or not to have the finished model with an open or closed hood section will often determine the answer. In the closed position, however clear the transparent sections of the razorback "greenhouse" are, there will be some distortion. The degree of detail visible through the bubbletop canopy of a P-47D is also limited due to the brace mechanism behind the pilot's seat, the headrest and in all versions, the notable curvature of the fuselage at that point.

It should be stressed at this juncture that the foregoing is intended for the enthusiastic beginner to do as the chapter heading says – to get started. Not for a moment would I suggest that the highly skilled builder who also intends to enter his model in a competition would want to skimp the cockpit, particularly bearing in mind that event judges invariably carry pen torches to probe the model's innards to see exactly how much has been put in – or left off.

ABOVE The only extra item destined for the P-47D kit was a harness from Eduard's set No. 49 001: Seatbelts USAF & USN WWII. These photo-etched belts have been pre-painted and are microscopically detailed.

covering relatively large areas of plastic with paint, although I note that the number of coats necessary for complete, in-depth coverage can be quite high, and the time it takes is not insubstantial either.

Having been totally in the hands of a succession of increasingly beat-up Badger and Aztec airbrushes in recent years, I've come to know my place. I spray how the brush wants to most of the time but hold the option of replacing the thing if it flatly refuses to comply after repeated cleaning and bathing in thinners. Stripping the brush right down to give it a thorough clean remains a last resort although many people won't do this on the grounds that it might not go back together correctly, thereby postponing completion of the model. You can actually get away with merely spraying through the old color and regularly washing the brush in thinners and/or a proprietary cleaner that comes in aerosol form.

Obviously, successful airbrushing requires the user to follow some cardinal rules, including using light shades before dark ones, and taking care when spraying silver or aluminum to clean the brush (even more thoroughly than usual) to avoid contamination of other colors.

The rapid amount of heat generated by the average compressor in about one hour's spraying is surprising. The model I currently use has a nasty tendency to jam if it becomes too hot but luckily gets going again when it has been allowed to cool down. As an alternative to a compressor, canned gas propellant will "drive" an airbrush: although it gives a high enough pressure to activate the brush, the pressure can vary. If the can has been stored for some time the contents can go flat, leading to uneven pressure and the need to constantly shake the contents into life. This on-off tendency alone soon makes people invest in a compressor. Those on the market are either universal, or intended for use with a certain brand of airbrush, the prices varying to suit different needs and the degree of features. These include a pressure regulator, a water trap and the capacity to operate more than one brush at a time, if necessary. Homemade compressors still figure in modeling, the advantage with this type being that extra features can be fitted for convenience and flexibility in spraying.

Whatever paint applicator system one employs, the difference an airbrush makes in obtaining a smooth finish to a model cannot be over-emphasized. That is not to imply that hand brushing no longer has a place in model

Building a model straight out of the box, using only what is provided by the manufacturer without any modification, has been legitimized by the International Plastic Modeling Society as a competition class in its own right: there could hardly be better proof of how high a standard today's kits have reached, such as the Tamiya P-47D shown. Above all, modeling should be an enjoyable, absorbing pastime, not a stress-ridden search to acquire every accessory on the market. Like football, which was once only a game, model making can become a high cost, angst-ridden, reputation-risking business. Don't ever let that happen to you!

AIR OR PAINTBRUSH?

There are still many modelers who have never quite mastered the art of spraying models with an airbrush, and who get along with the time honored hand-held brush. I suspect however that such individuals are in the minority, particularly if there is a penchant for the larger scale kit. An airbrush is almost essential for making, as a set of fine sables is indispensable, ideal for bringing out intricate detail in the aircraft cockpit, tires, wheel hubs and engines, to name but a few areas. Running thinned paint into panel lines to emphasize wear is another important function of small brushes in typically 00, 0 and 01 sizes. Brushes are also necessary to place decals correctly and where necessary, to apply a coat or two of softening agent.

CHOOSING A FINISH

To return to our P-47D: having sprayed or hand painted all areas of the interior that will be visible once the two fuselage halves are attached, and completed the cockpit, our model is a further step nearer to completion. By this stage a choice has to be made on the final color scheme, based either on an overall camouflaged effect or natural metal finish (NMF). It is not that unpainted USAAF fighters ever remained in pristine conditioned compared to their contemporaries in olive green and neutral gray camouflage paint – it is just that the weathering effect was somewhat different. From the modeler's viewpoint, a poor joint that can be hidden by several coats of Olive Drab will not be quite so easy to disguise with a plain finish.

Aluminum or silver paint has slightly different properties to the pigment in all other color shades and some model paints are specially formulated to be lighter for application by airbrush. The coats will therefore be thinner, allowing the model's surface detail – or scratches – to show through that much more easily. Care and patience should result in hardly any bad joints being visible – but the old adage that if things can go wrong, they invariably will, applies as much to modeling as any other human endeavor – probably more so for some people!

ADHESIVES

At this point we need to look at the range of adhesives available. The most popular are the liquid cement type marketed by such firms as Humbrol, and heavier duty tube-cement type. This latter is also sold by commercial suppliers and model kit companies and is most widely used for firmly bonding joints such as wing sections to the fuselage – anywhere that a stronger join is necessary. Used less today than it once was, tube cement would, if you are clumsy, craze the plastic surface. On the one hand this may assure a better bond as the two plastic faces tend to melt into each other, but the drawback is that the cement can lie on the

surfaces, stay pliable and bulge out of the joint when two surfaces are mated up under pressure. As with all aspects of this hobby, a light touch when applying the cement will pay dividends. Help is at hand with Revell's Contacta cement, which comes in a square flexipack with a slim nozzle applicator. This metal extension tube is ideal for getting adhesive into those inaccessible corners where an extra drop or two will ensure that nothing comes loose, particularly inside the fuselage.

Otherwise, liquid cement will cope with most modeling tasks. Applied sparingly, it leaves virtually no trace on the plastic surface (although it certainly will mark the plastic

ABOVE The Eduard belts were mounted on top of the rail behind the pilot's seat, representing the way they looped over and behind this bar. The brown headrest received a wash of thinned Raw Umber oil paint to make it look more leather-like. Tiny silver chips were added to the seat, the floor and the rear bulkhead using a silver pencil.

BELOW The P-47D's raised ribbed flooring is very impressive and free of any molding imperfections.

if accidentally spilled) and without the "stringing" effect that tube cement can create.

Liquid adhesive is applied with a small brush – often supplied with the bottle it comes in – and works by capillary action so that it creeps quickly along the smallest of joints. Its general non-staining properties make it ideal for attaching clear parts to solid sections, such as cockpit canopies and formation lights. It has the slight disadvantage of sometimes drying so quickly on contact with air that repeat applications are necessary. This type of adhesive, which has all but revolutionized plastic modeling, is becoming more efficient and substances that come into the plastic-weld (a liquid adhesive is marketed by Microscale under that name) category can occasionally be used to close up gaps that would otherwise require filling and filing – two chores that I, and I suspect many others, dislike intensely.

Personally, I never use enough adhesive. Over the years, and maybe remembering the days when models were marked by the amount of dried adhesive one could actually see in the joints, I've taken the warning "use glue sparingly" rather to heart. But today the range of adhesives to cover all modeling tasks is wide and you can chose the one that suits, a combination of polystyrene cement and liquid adhesive being ideal for most modeling tasks. If all else fails, cyanoacrylate (superglue) will surely do the job. The one drawback in using it is that, lacking the flexibility of other model adhesives, you have to get the positioning right first time and closely monitor the drying out process.

To ensure that the glued parts hold together along their entire length, wrap elastic bands or adhesive tape around them, check continually that no slippage has meanwhile occurred between left and right or top and bottom halves, and leave them to dry thoroughly. This is where a useful and simple modeling tool comes into its own – attach ordinary household clothes pegs along the wing leading and trailing edges. This can be preferable to elastic

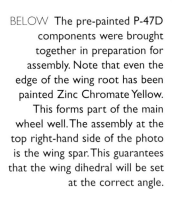

BELOW The pre-painted P-47D components were brought together in preparation for assembly. Note that even the edge of the wing root has been painted Zinc Chromate Yellow. This forms part of the main wheel well. The assembly at the top right-hand side of the photo is the wing spar. This guarantees that the wing dihedral will be set at the correct angle.

bands, which might snag an *in situ* aerial or other delicate component. On a P-47 kit you may for example, have had to fit two carriers for the eight wing guns within the two wing halves prior to gluing. The blast tubes will of course stick out of each leading edge and any heavy-handedness in wrapping the rubber bands tightly around the wing might risk snapping them off, so a humble peg or two comes in very handy.

For detail painting, decal application or tasks such as anchoring aerial wires securely, a desk-mounted clamp may be the answer. Set at any given angle with a number of jaws to hold the model rigid, these may be used in conjunction with special daylight lighting (bulbs or specially-designed lamps) and hand-held or rigid magnifiers, if required.

Special adhesives will be necessary if your modeling branches out into using brass etch and other customizing accessories. A range of cyanoacrylates are available from specialist suppliers, the adhesives sold for model making often having been specially formulated to get good results from bonding otherwise incompatible materials such as copper, plastic and resin. The best guide to determining the correct adhesive for the job you have in mind is to check guides that appear from time to time in the modeling press, although the mail order houses will be happy to advise on what product will best suit your particular requirements. The accessory itself (or the retailer who stocks it) should also provide some guidance in this respect.

YOUR OWN WAY

One reason for great care in checking wing and tailplane alignment and making sure they will indeed fit well without need for much post adhesive rubbing down is that it is perfectly possible to digress considerably from the instruction sheet. By this I mean completing all the work on the P-47 fuselage including painting and maybe applying the decals before assembling and attaching the wings.

Any work on the fuselage, where most of the decals and detail painting are grouped, will be far easier without the wings and tailplanes sticking out at right angles and getting in the way. You may also want to postpone attaching the engine cowling for a similar reason. Masking for painting will thus be far easier and should there be any need for hand painting, i.e. as an alternative to persuading a decal to lay down around the nose ring of a P-47 cowling, then working on an uncluttered fuselage will provide much more freedom of movement. It should be emphasized here that before tackling the fuselage the fit of the other parts will have been thoroughly checked for good alignment and trimmed where necessary.

Once you are sure that everything will fit well when you are ready for final assembly, the wings may be attached to the fuselage. When this is carried out, over half the job will have been done. More time will be saved if you pre-spray the wings and tailplane and any other parts when you apply the fuselage color: the importance of conducting several dry runs cannot be emphasized enough. Check again

that the wing to fuselage alignment is correct and the dihedral angle is right. If so, each undercarriage leg can be located and set at the correct forward-rake angle, taking care to view these from head-on and from each side to ensure that the toe-in is also as per the original aircraft. It is very important to consult a reference photo or two for the correct "hang" of the undercarriage legs, as kit instructions can be vague and three-view plans simply wrong about this detail. Also make sure that both oleo legs are in line on both sides. The legs can be left to dry out by suspending the model inside an upturned box lid (or two paint tins of equal height). Any suitable lightweight object can be used as props to support the fuselage and ensure that there is no movement of the legs while the adhesive dries out.

Once the undercarriage angle has been set correctly, work can be carried out on any extra detail such as brake or hydraulic lines that need to be run from the wheel hub up into the well. While wartime fighters were not nearly so complex in this area as their modern day counterparts, any small items you add to the model should have logical anchorage points

inside the well. Sway braces to keep the inboard undercarriage doors in place in the down position also need to be attended to, although these will usually be part of the kit.

When the oleos have dried firmly, attach the wheel well doors that have been pre-painted, and fit the wheels to their oleo pins. Many kits provide a choice between hub blanking plates or "open" hub spokes. If the kit you have chosen does not, and the chosen P-47 subject is a late-war example, wheel hubs with the spokes visible might need to be found from elsewhere. This sort of detail is often hard to check: aircraft wheels usually had hub plates but in some theaters of war the ground crew regularly left them off if they were prone to a build up of mud. Then there is the factor of different wheel hubs being fitted to later production aircraft – but you won't find many P-47 references going into such detail, so the reliable yardstick of "model what you see" holds good in this instance. Photographs are once again the most reliable guides and it is pleasing to see that modern kits (and decal sheets) are increasingly including reference photos on their instructions.

Wheels on fighter kits have only recently matured to the point where we get treads and "flats" for an aircraft under load. This is a definite plus on behalf of the manufacturers but do check that the degree of load is not excessive to the point where if the tires were as flat as shown, the aircraft would not roll. Many kits still have "round" wheels, in which case make your own flat area on each tire. Also of importance is to check the cross section of the wheels supplied in the kit. While things are much better in this respect than they used to be in the days when tires were generally too thin when viewed from head on, manufacturers can still slip up. In addition, the tires should have the correct tread pattern: a close study of photographs and manuals reveals noticeable differences over the lengthy production lifetime of an aircraft such as the P-47.

Apart from references to the fitting of low-pressure tires (not necessarily on P-47s), not even the manufacturers of tires were closely identified with supplying the wartime aircraft companies, Republic in this instance. The household-name manufacturers of today were doing just the same during the war. But how many people can state categorically "P-47 wheels were always fitted with Goodyear tires"? If so, how much did the patterns vary? Wartime US combat aircraft did not, to my knowledge, have different tire compositions and tread patterns for different operating conditions such as the variety fitted to Formula 1 racing cars, for example – if only life was that simple!

So, in dealing with this kind of vexed question, never assume anything; just give the model wheels to match those in the reference photos as closely as possible. You may say that nobody will notice, which may be true – but once you get an eye for these things, you at least know what looks better on your own model.

Before leaving the subject of P-47 wheels, individual examples of the earlier machines sported a variety of designs on the hub plates. These included white stars, numbers, different segments painted in squadron colors and even a reproduction of the unit insignia – take a close look to see what can be detected in photographs. You may well come across a nice little extra detail that can be added to further enhance the model. For example, on late-war P-47Ns, identity on flight lines was enhanced by repeating the aircraft number on the mainwheel covers.

FINISHING TOUCHES
Final detailing of your P-47 includes locating the propeller, running an aerial wire from the radio mast to the fin, and attending to any ordnance you wish the model to carry.

P-47 propellers had at least four different blade shapes but the most important thing is the source of the manufacturer because their

LEFT After assembly, a tiny seam line was visible on the P-47D's lower fuselage. This was filled with Mr Surfacer and sanded lightly with fine abrasive paper. This was the only filling and sanding required on the entire kit.

ABOVE Aeromaster sheet AMD48-71 includes spectacular markings for a hard-working P-47D in natural metal. The decals performed perfectly, with no carrier film visible even before a sealing coat over the markings. The metallic surface was wetted with Micro Set before the decals were applied. A thin coat of Micro Sol setting solution was brushed over the decals to ensure that they settled right into panel lines. Step by step photographs on achieving the natural metal finish on this model will be dealt with in Chapter 6: Special Techniques.

product was noticeably different. Does the reference indicate the Curtiss Electric type (quite pointed, with blade cuffs) or a Hamilton Standard, which was broader without cuffs? The hubs were also different, the Curtiss type having a more pointed front end while the HS had a rounded, more domed appearance.

While there may even be a choice of propeller in your kit, the radio aerial will be a standard fitting. Check that it is of the right height and strong enough to support the aerial wire. Using thin fishing line or stretched sprue, add the wire stretched between the mast and the fin. A small drop of tube cement should be enough to replicate the condensers, which are often the only items visible in photos to prove that there was a wire there at all. Anchor the wire firmly with superglue.

Selecting the drop tanks, bombs or rockets your Thunderbolt carries will depend a lot on the wartime date. Different drop tanks and ordnance were introduced progressively on wartime Thunderbolts but kit manufacturers get carried a way sometimes and throw in all

the bombs, tanks and rockets they can fit on the sprues. Faced with all of this, the novice may not realize the stress limitations that prevented the entire lot being loaded at once!

Various sub-types of P-47 – and most other fighter types – were built and/or modified to take various types of stores, so some familiarity with serial numbers of the variants soon becomes a necessity. Even armed with the information that explains on which sub-types a particular item of ordnance was carried, field modifications to update older aircraft can hold hidden pitfalls for the modeler. In some combat units older Thunderbolts rarely gave way entirely to new replacements, as there was an acute shortage in some areas. When you are aware that it was not unknown for a front-line group to receive a half dozen P-47 sub-variants at one time, the notion that for example, the bubbletops replaced the razorbacks is, as a general statement, far from true. This brings the record of actual events, places and dates into the realm of modeling more than might initially be realized.

INSIGNIA INSIGHTS

Having decided on the markings our P-47 will get it is time to choose the decals, either one of the options provided in the kit, or a commercial sheet with several alternative subjects, such as the Aeromaster sheet shown on page 28. The latter will not always include the national insignia, which is supplied on the kit sheet, so these should be cut as closely as possible and applied. Now comes another of those near-impossible questions regarding markings. Prior to D-Day all tactical P-47s had an additional 55 or 60 inch (the diameter of the star on blue roundel) size national insignia under the right wing – but when was it removed? There does not seem to have been a published order covering this requirement, and the modeler will note both marking styles remaining in use for some time after D-Day. In fact he often won't actually see the underside of the subject aircraft clearly as even good quality reference photographs are invariably in deep shadow if they have been through a reproduction process. And of course, the only reference photo you have may have been taken from the "wrong" side anyway. The fact that the national insignia appears on the underside of the starboard wing is no indicator of whether is also appeared on the port side.

The point of all this in modeling terms is that the largest size underwing national

insignia on P-47s was painted on before the pylons were attached. The kit instructions should be a guide to this and the decal sheet may include the extra insignia with a couple of spots to indicate where the pylon pins go – but don't bank on this always being the case, particularly if the kit decal options are not used. All the modeler can do in this instance is assume that in the European Theater after a given date an 8th or 9th Air Force P-47D will have had the additional insignia applied.

The problem of determining P-47 markings at a certain date with total accuracy is somewhat compounded by replacement aircraft. Most groups suffered losses during combat missions in 1944–45 and both new production and older aircraft were received. A great many P-47Ds, both razorbacks and bubbletops, were passed on to the 9th Air Force by the 8th Air Force as its groups converted to Mustangs but I don't know the full extent of repainting after these latter machines were refurbished at depots. Photographic evidence would however appear to indicate that a pristine exterior for tactical aircraft was the last thing to trouble AAF planners at that time.

The P-47 combat groups themselves worked under the pretext of "if it isn't broken, don't fix it": photos show razorbacks in service at the end of the war complete with their

LEFT A thin coat of flat varnish was sprayed over the model to tone down the contrast between the panels and to blend the decals with the model's surface. The kit's canopy fits quite securely without glue. The windscreen is recessed into the forward fuselage, and the sliding canopy section snaps into position, effectively locking the windscreen into place.

unit's final color recognition markings and as one would expect, a pretty beat up appearance. Invariably the shiny, recent replacement bubbletops can be noted on the same flight line – all of which makes modeling the American wartime fighters a fascinating if occasionally frustrating pastime.

Lastly, our P-47 needs fuel to get to the target and something to attack it with. Here again reference to color photos will confirm the shade of paint used on the various types of drop tank, but there are guidelines. If we take the standard cylindrical 108-gal. type, the ruling was that those manufactured in the UK were painted gray while those tanks from US production were NMF. Anomalies occur when photos indicate a darker shade of color on tanks as these were sometimes taken from aircraft and stores dating from the time that camouflage was in use. Another reason to check those dates.

As to the design of tank hanging under your subject model, photos (and experience) will soon enable you to sort out the cylindrical from the flat type, even if the aircraft is viewed in profile and the tank is hard to see in those shadows mentioned before. The least confusion is provided by a teardrop-shaped 75-gal. tank.

When it comes to adding ordnance, the type and color of bombs carried by P-47s must be taken into consideration. Thankfully, model kits have finally reached a level of sophistication that has made toolmakers largely stop the practice of incorporating the rack into one half of the bomb. Such molding-in makes

model kit bombs look less than authentic but if this old type matches the size you need, simply cut the pins off the "smooth" half and stick two male/female halves together. You'll need to have several kits or a healthy spares box to get enough male or female halves, but this is preferable to hacking an integral rack off the thing.

Also irksome are bombs with grooves in the surface to enable them to attach firmly. Once again, many recent kits contain correctly scaled attachment points for bombs and drop tanks, complete with tiny screw down clamps which were usually angled inwards from the carrier rack. I feel that pins designed to penetrate the surface of kit bombs is all right provided that the scale is correct. Firm attachment of ordnance can be tricky, especially if the model needs to be moved around, so an extra drop of cement may be very necessary to keep them in place.

Fortunately, many of today's fighter kits also provide separate bomb fins. In a continuing attempt to obtain true scale accuracy the manufacturers are achieving very acceptable thin sections in these tiny components. But there is a limit to what the molding process will stand. If you bear in mind that no plastic bomb (or rocket) used on a P-47 kit (in any scale) would look out of place with fins the thickness of a piece of typing paper, you'll quickly reject all but the very best and very thinnest of kit components. This will unfortunately clean out almost all your plastic armament stock because so many bombs have in the past had fins that were far too thick for scale accuracy. Re-cutting them all from plastic card is the real answer but in suggesting this I do not dismiss the complexity of the task, especially when dealing with bombs fitted with those intricate box-type fins. If bomb improvement proves to be too time-consuming, there's no reason not to delay finishing the rest of the kit – you can always detail the bomb(s) later. It's not a bad idea to reserve painting and marking of bombs and other items of ordnance until such time as you can complete enough for several models. Focusing on this one aspect of model making does breed familiarity with colors and markings. Setting aside the bomb(s) may also be advantageous if you are awaiting delivery of the latest brass-etch accessory with which to detail the fins and add arming wires and those tiny fusing propellers.

Another job in this area of the kit is to check the detail of the wing racks. As is obvious from photos, P-47 racks were some of the largest ever fitted to US aircraft. With their prominent sway braces they were also always covered in stenciled instructions, these being supplied as decals in many current kits. The later type of P-47 rack also had a lever arm at the rear to push the bomb away from the wing. This may need to be added to your kit.

Referring back a minute to the underwing insignia – if you are modeling a P-47 operating in the ETO and the kit is one of the old ones from Monogram, the wing racks might have to be cut off. This is a pain but the option chosed may require you to apply the extra insignia under the rack and to detail the rack. Alternatively, simply cut the national insignia decal and set the bars inboard of the racks on both sides. This will also need to be done on several 1/72-scale Thunderbolts that have their racks molded as part of the wing too.

EXPLOSIVE COLORS

References for the colors and markings of US wartime ordnance are rare, so to speak, as there are few handy guides to what is an overlooked subject. Even the massive camouflage and markings tomes do not delve into the paint schemes of air weaponry to any extent. Fortunately, the books devoted to the aircraft in question can provide us with such information and much else of interest to the modeler. The best sources are the widely available books of color photos, and magazine articles. Specialist modeling journals have covered the subject of bomb colors over the years, but in case the reader does not have access to any of these, the standard USAAF bomb colors are listed on page 114 of this book.

BELOW A three-quarter rear view of the completed Tamiya P-47D Razorback.

CHAPTER 2

REFERENCE SOURCES

Modelers of wartime USAAF fighter aircraft are arguably better off than those whose interests are centered on virtually any other aspect of aviation, in that the amount of available reference material is enormous. Most people will start with a few books, approaching the subject either from the modeling end per se or from a study of the historical aspects – campaigns, combat operations, special missions, biographies of pilots and unit histories. Fortunately, all such references will invariably contain photographs of relevant aircraft in monochrome or color, and possibly, a page or two of color illustrations in the form of side-view profiles.

Recent decades have also seen the rise of numerous "overview" books which detail American wartime fighters in varying degrees of depth, illustrated with photographs and schematic drawings. Although the enthusiast will most likely have purchased one or more of these as new when they first appeared or as second-hand volumes since, he will pretty soon learn that they tend to be continually repackaged – like some kits – and contain the same hackneyed color profiles and cutaways. These large-format, heavily illustrated tomes do however have some value for checking basic

dimensions and so forth, providing that the data contained therein is reliable.

Every current monthly or quarterly aviation magazine, and many books aiming at a high volume readership and a share of a crowded market, tend to include color profiles which vary in quality to a significant degree. Often there is also noticeable duplication of subject, for out of all the thousands of USAAF fighters that saw combat, only a certain percentage had all their markings fully recorded. These have been illustrated as side-view profiles many times, simply because although the potential variation is vast, the number of aircraft about which complete details are known seems to expand only slowly. There is also the reality that publishers will often re-use existing material rather than bear the cost of commissioning new artwork! This situation has in the past led to bookshops being crowded out with "pot boilers" that should largely be ignored by the enthusiast seeking to expand his horizons.

For these and other reasons, many books on USAAF aircraft contain variations on the same old theme; "favorite" P-51D Mustang schemes such as the 361st Fighter Group's 44-14181/E2-D "Detroit Miss," and 44-13926/E2-S, various Thunderbolts of the 56th Fighter Group

RIGHT Aircraft profiles can often provide inspiration for a modeler. This attractive rendering of a P-40L Warhawk was created digitally by Thierry Dekker. It was used as the box art on AMtech's 1/48-scale P-40F/L kit.

Wolfpack, Medal of Honor winner William Shomo's F-6D 44-72505 "The Flying Undertaker/Snooks 5th" and Charles MacDonald's P-38L "Putt Putt Maru" to name but a few, are still regulars in modern books on the subject – as they are bound to be, integral as they are to the story of the respective aircraft and the operations they flew. These and other well-known fighters have also had wide exposure as kit and commercial decal subjects, the drawback for the modern modeler being that these color schemes have already been used by countless other kit builders all over the world.

In the unlikely event that no alternative scheme can be found, a representative collection of models of 8th Air Force Mustangs will probably include these hackneyed old favorites. Modelers with access to better data will have shunned these well-known schemes in favor of something fresh. The situation arises whereby the modeler is able to complete a dozen kits in the markings of other aircraft in a given group after publication of a new, well-illustrated unit history.

Obviously the artwork in some books, either airbrush rendered or computer sourced, is only as good as the individual artist's references, his interpretation and the technical difficulties involved in reproducing digital images accurately on the printed page. It is true to say that the subject of US fighter colors has expanded significantly in terms of fresh schemes in the last ten years or so. While we still see the favorites, they increasingly share the single or double-page spreads of books and magazines, as well as decal sheets, with less familiar subjects. It is these that offer the opportunity for new modeling projects.

FIGHTERS ON FILM

Another welcome phenomenon of recent years has been the increase in the number of wartime images, both printed and on film, in full color. Many of the stills that have been reproduced were diligently unearthed across the USA by the late Jeff Ethell and it is to him and like-minded individuals that the modeling fraternity should be grateful for a whole area of new data. It took decades, but those long-held color views have finally seen publication. Books such as *Fighter Command: The History of Aircraft Nose Art*, *War Eagles in Original Color* and *Pacific War Eagles* have added immensely to our knowledge of fighter camouflage and markings as actually applied "in the field."

Color photography has brought confirmation (as well as contradiction) regarding the details

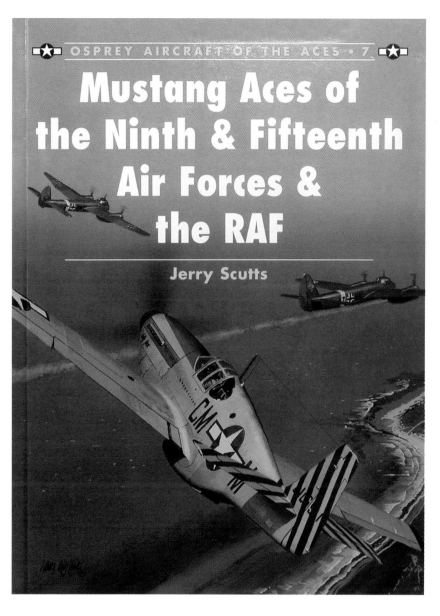

of certain aircraft, subjects which, we always assumed in our ignorance, were shot only in monochrome. There is no reference as good as a color photo, however poorly it may have traveled in the 60 years since it was snapped. Only through this can we prove that what everyone thought was a black tail stripe was in fact painted in red or dark blue.

Among the most valuable features of color photos is confirmation of the shades used for nose artwork names and images. It is well known that USAAF front line units used combinations of red, yellow and white – in other words the most visible colours – to personalize their machines, but it is pleasing to have the fact confirmed. Reds and yellows are notoriously difficult to determine from monochrome photos and some individual aircraft schemes have been the subject of guesswork for years.

Most experienced modelers will use the standard package of monotone photographs,

ABOVE Osprey Publishing offers a wide selection of books in their Aircraft of the Aces series. These include historical notes, operational descriptions, many wartime photos, line drawings and profiles.

1067

P-47 Thunderbolt

in action

Aircraft Number 67
squadron/signal publications

written evidence, plans and color drawings, plus some color photos. Unfortunately it is not always possible to extract all the information required from a single volume. There are books that indeed trap almost all there is to know between two covers but this is hardly ever the case in regard to widely used aircraft such as US Army fighters, so vast is the subject. Taking all war theaters together, fighter color schemes run into the hundreds if not thousands.

Another fascinating area of markings that has been given the hardback book treatment in recent years is nose art. There are various titles available but for the subject under review *US Fighter Nose Art* by John and Donna Campbell and Jeff Ethell's *The History of Aircraft Nose Art* are both indispensable guides to the subject. The latter volume not only shows the reader the original calendar art from which many of the pin-ups stemmed, but some biographical notes on the artists themselves.

The Campbell tome is handily divided into theaters and although not always providing as much caption detail as hoped, the book can set an enthusiast on the trail of the rest of the aircraft, as of course only the front end is usually depicted. One exception is the artwork widely applied to the cockpit doors on P-39 Airacobras, a fighter type that remains to be researched in depth to determine further details, including in some cases the RAF serial number. The question is: did the aircraft have one applied or not? A model could be incomplete without it.

The variety of published references outlined above provides the modeler setting up a library with most of what is needed to complete a number of plastic kits. There are many very good value titles on the market and although a high price will often be asked for imported books, this additional cost is offset by the fact that full color books do not appear every week.

In Europe there has been a steady flow of published data on USAAF fighters despite the fact that some favored series such as Profiles and Aircam have long since disappeared. Osprey has done much to redress any perceived lack of an informative, English-language aviation book series with their highly acclaimed Aircraft of the Aces, Combat Aircraft and Production to Front Line series.

Some of the titles covering aces have presented many hitherto unknown markings details to delight the model maker. The various authors of these titles also do their best to unearth photographs to back up the color profiles (which are usually of exceptionally high quality), as this is ultra-important to the modeler. Types such as the P-40 Warhawk have received little prior coverage with regard to the most successful pilots who flew them after the American Volunteer Group had completed its stint in China and Burma. Carl Molesworth's two titles covering the P-40 units operating in the CBI and MTO are the most comprehensive yet on the markings of a very significant airplane.

A perennial favorite with the modeler, the P-40 has never looked back since reliable data was first released on the early models flown by the famed Flying Tigers. Few other aircraft markings have made such an impression as the AVG sharkmouth: perpetuated far beyond the products of Curtiss, these double rows of deadly white teeth were first popularized by No. 112 Squadron RAF. Not that color profiles have been very kind to the aircraft of the AVG: the latest research shows that for years the colors, particularly of the undersides, were wrongly assumed to be closer to those used by the RAF than was actually the case. This is another reason not to rely on data, particularly artists' impressions, published in books some 30 years ago. Always check if there is something more up to date.

As a general point on color drawing references, it may also be found that the artist has cleaned up the aircraft for the purposes of clarity, so the importance of reference photos to check this and other points cannot be over-emphasized. As with pretty much every other aspect of research, in time the modeler will come to know which references, authors and artists to rely on and those to treat with some caution.

AMERICAN LEAD

As far as core references to fighter units and markings go, I don't know what I'd have done without the magnificent Air Force Story series by Kenn Rust. Published in the 1970s by Historical Aviation Album in the US they covered all US air units serving overseas except the 11th Air Force in the Aleutians. Before they appeared we were floundering, not knowing that much about the order of fighter color schemes and to which group aircraft belonged. Some gaps in our knowledge remain to this day but 90 per cent of this type of data is there in nine volumes. In some instances they revealed details of units we previously knew little or nothing about – and have had little else since. If you don't have these titles, try to find them if you can – the search will be well rewarded.

In the US, Squadron/Signal continue to extend the In Action series to include ever more unusual types. For the modeler of the P-47, two titles by Ernie McDowell are excellent. Dividing the aircraft's combat operations into Europe and the MTO and the CBI/Pacific theaters, he shows the sequential markings of all front-line units, backed by the usual top quality artwork for which these books are renowned.

Having taken over distribution of the Detail & Scale series, Squadron/Signal is also currently offering even more titles of interest to the modeler of USAAF fighters, with recent titles on the P-39 and P-40 to add to those previously released. Detail & Scale have, in what I feel to be a detrimental move, cut back on the kit review section from some of their latest titles. These reviews were not intended to be anything other than basic plus and minus points of kits but they did cover the entire scale range – very useful if the subject aircraft was a relatively new type in modeling terms and the individual was in some doubt as to which is the most accurate kit and the best value for money.

WarbirdTech is the generic name of yet another popular US series edited by Frederick A Johnson, which has a slightly different approach in that each title contains a wealth of technical drawings copied from official servicing manuals, the sort of visual data that is invaluable to modelers. Sectional breakdowns of areas such as undercarriage operation, gun sight mountings, ammunition stowage and canopy construction are but a few of the informative visual feasts that this series presents. In addition, WarbirdTech volumes include a regular color photo section that usually brings to light some fresh markings schemes to add to the bank of knowledge on the type in question.

Other gaps in the single-type coverage of wartime aircraft are rapidly being filled by

BELOW Squadron's Walk Around series focuses on the details of the particular aircraft subject. The photographic subjects are usually a combination of operational aircraft and museum models.

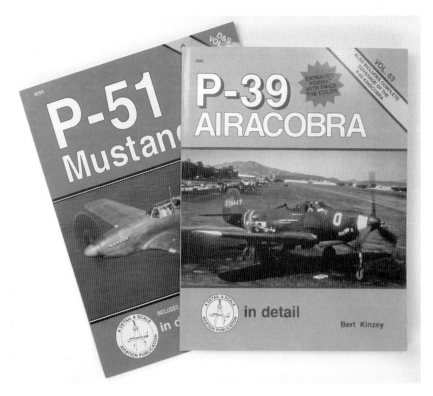

ABOVE Bert Kinzey's Detail & Scale series of books are a great resource for modelers. As the name of the series implies, the subject aircraft is examined in detail with plenty of photographs and scale drawings. Recent titles include a generous selection of color photos.

status have often been subject to a certain number of internal and exterior modifications to enable them to incorporate modern avionics and meet current air safety standards. And while new blade aerials or repositioned D/F loops are obvious enough, the fact that the cockpit may have been cleaned up compared to wartime examples may be overlooked. Such modernization is most obvious in the area immediately in front of the pilot. The intrusive, often bulky gun sight, which could make a nasty mess of the pilot's face in the event of a crash landing, was a wartime necessity. Today it is not and the sight and its heavy-duty mounting bracket have invariably been removed.

Cockpit instrumentation has also been given greater readability by being set in a panel in contrasting colors, usually lighter than the universal black that was used originally. Instruments have also been rearranged for enhanced readability. Wartime black-faced instruments on a black board can indeed be difficult to read and the changes are understandable – but authentic they are not.

Wartime fighter cockpits also had a plethora of knobs and levers sticking out at angles. Although they were vital to a combat role, modern day warbirds are long past their days of action and restorers do have a tendency to remove items that no longer have any useful function. This may be to save weight, because some items of equipment are unavailable, or to allow the pilot to exit the cockpit that little bit faster, should a mishap occur – all very understandable, but not to be slavishly copied on a scale model purporting to represent an accurate wartime-vintage fighter. Be wary of areas that might for various reasons be non-standard.

Static museum exhibits are in a different category. Aircraft that are no longer required to fly can be fully restored down to the last rivet and bolt with absolute authenticity. One only has to see a photo record of such restoration work being undertaken to know that what you see is totally faithful to the original. Museum staff also go to great lengths to ensure that all the colors of parts are correct, so modern aircraft rebuild projects could in some cases be the best reference available to the model maker.

numerous profiles from Eastern Europe. These books vary in quality but have the advantage of a modest price tag and generally good content, including pages of multi-view drawings, which are very useful for modeling purposes. The detail these titles go into is extremely impressive in some instances and as the contents are heavily biased towards the visual, the language barrier is not the drawback it may at first seem. The continuing proliferation of these titles would suggest that model makers eagerly seek them out.

GENUINE DATA?

Another recent addition to the coverage of World War 2 fighters are the Walk Around series published by Squadron/Signal, and the comparable Aero Detail. Both are heavily illustrated, high quality series, the latter imported from Japan. Chock full of close-up photos of nearly every inch of the subject aircraft, these books can be invaluable in determining the exact size and shape of items such as slats, slots, hinges, rods, grilles, seat harnesses and many other details that are not readily visible in photos of the full aircraft. The one reservation I would pass on about such books is that the color photography, magnificent as it is, sometimes takes its subject matter from flyable warbirds or static museum examples, rather than a stock original.

There can be numerous differences between the two: historic aircraft refurbished to flyable

COLOR REFERENCE

Any self-respecting modeler's reference library will include one or more of the color-guide type book which purports to be a complete A to Z of USAAC/USAAF/USAF markings and camouflage colors in transition from the late-1930s to post 1947. I personally find some of these books disappointing, as while they will exhaustively list – and indeed show in full-page illustrations – the exact dimensions of the US national insignia, list all known color specs and perhaps provide color chips, they tend to skip the numerous exceptions to the rule that make this subject so fascinating. In the real world things were often rather different to what was officially stipulated, as many modelers will know.

In terms of color guides, Dana Bell's work will be all many modelers need to obtain a comprehensive overview of what is a vast subject. An acknowledged expert in his field, Dana has been delving into paint schemes and markings for years but he would be the first to admit that there is still more to be unearthed. What he has published so far is admirable in its depth and scope.

Equally good but in an entirely different format were the Camouflage & Markings booklets written by Roger Freeman for Ducimus Books of the UK some years ago. Covering the main US combat types in great depth (considering the limited number of pages) these publications are also invaluable for checking insignia dimensions, styles of serial numbers and code letters, and other details that always seem to need looking up, such as the dates when the US national insignia was supposed to have changed from a red outline to blue.

That this directive was not complied with overnight is inevitable when one considers the magnitude of the task of remarking hundreds of aircraft; actual speed of compliance at unit level sometimes depended on the perceived importance of the new marking directive. The complaint from the Pacific Theater that at a distance, any red in the insignia could be mistaken for a Japanese *Hinomaru* (or "meatball") hardly applied in Europe. When the paint shops got around to it, the red outline was temporarily overpainted in a dark blue that is often visible in photos. On the other hand, some paint directives were immediately complied with. The sheer volume of work undertaken on June 5, 1944 to apply AEAF black and white stripes to every US fighter, medium bomber, transport and liaison aircraft in England was rarely if ever equaled.

The Ducimus series had unfortunately a few gaps. No P-39 or P-40 titles were included in the USAAF section: while we're on the subject of color a few notes pertaining to these types are relevant. It is surprising, for instance,

just how many P-40s in US service in 1942–44 were camouflaged in British-style shadow shading. Various references will mislead on this subject when artists, referring to overly dark photos, interpret the top surface shade as overall Olive Drab. True, the camouflage took a battering in the tropical climate in which many P-40s operated but there are enough photos about for this kind of detail to be double-checked.

A similar situation existed with Airacobras, which in many cases not only carried British camouflage but serial numbers as well. These were relatively rare on P-40s, but both types reached American hands via depots after having been painted at the factories following Ministry of Aircraft Production patterns. This leads us into another gray (or should that be green and brown) area regarding the actual shades. American paints were used to finish many hundreds of P-39s and P-40s ordered on British contracts, so some variation in relation to the paints applied to aircraft built in England will be noted.

Several widely reproduced color photos from the early to mid-war period will help match model paints to the correct hues, the early "sand and spinach" scheme being accompanied by the "desert scheme" of dark earth and middle stone. Light and dark brown shades later met USAAF "desert pink" to cloud the issue further. Many P-40s operating in the MTO had two-tone camouflage but sorting out the exact shades can sometimes be difficult.

The above comments regarding variation in paint shades apply equally to the camouflage on P-40s in other theaters, particularly the CBI. Aircraft tended weather to the point that determining the exact demarcation of colors at this distance in time, often from poor quality photographs, can be a near impossibility. Throw in the odd reference to the use of three top surface shades (a probable comment on US Olive Drab used for patch-up purposes) and the confusion deepens. The problem is, as ever, the preponderance of monochrome photos as the primary reference source to wartime aircraft; all the modeler can therefore do is to bear in mind but not be totally swayed by pre-determined, set-in-stone patterns and directives regarding paint application. What the reference photo indicates may bear no resemblance to any official order.

As black and white photos can also vary widely in quality the modeler can only aim to reproduce exactly what he sees, warts and all. Bearing in mind the colors in vogue at the time and in the place, a model can look quite

ABOVE The Japanese Aero Detail series is another good source of information for modelers. The aircraft plans included in each volume are especially useful. USAAF fighters covered in this series so far include the P-47 Thunderbolt and P-51 Mustang.

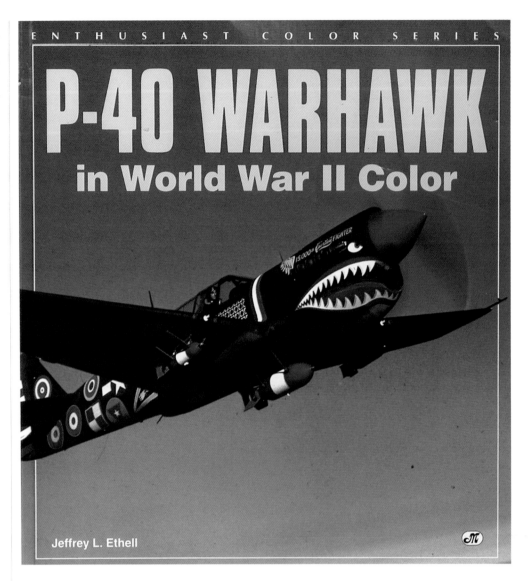

ENTHUSIAST COLOR SERIES

P-40 WARHAWK
in World War II Color

Jeffrey L. Ethell

exotic in its broadly interpreted camouflage. Unfortunately, the upper surfaces of real fighters are (unlike models) rarely photographed from above and behind to show the full camouflage pattern.

To return to the books, most of us know that when a highly desirable new reference title appears on the market it is far better to buy sooner rather than later. Such volumes vary notoriously in the size of their print runs and if you defer your purchase, the demand for the first edition may be so high that you find yourself waiting around for a reprint. There is, in some cases, no guarantee that this will appear and you are reduced to scouring the second-hand shops, or stalls at book fairs and air shows. The last resort may be the specialist dealer's list. But if the book was so popular the first time around, you may wait years for a copy to turn up.

The antidote to all this is to commit to a steady book purchasing plan to avoid disappointment. All aspects of aviation history

have a handful of groundbreaking titles that are at the core of any collection although these do not appear very frequently. Authors of such works of reference need to put in years of research in order to complete their manuscripts, which does at least give the buyer a breathing space!

USEFUL UNIT HISTORIES

One area of special interest to the individual studying USAAF fighter operations is the unit history. Often put together by one or more ex-flight or groundcrew veterans of the unit in question, these books have one thing in common – high prices. The quality, unfortunately, tends to vary considerably from photo-packed excellence to volumes that are very modest with very few illustrations of use in model making. On the positive side, the information and photos may be quite unique and as we are losing World War 2 servicemen at an alarming rate due to the passage of time, whatever they commit to print has some value. Their modest effort at recording how it was, at least from their personal standpoint, can never be repeated in quite the same way. Another reason for buying while you can.

Unit histories are published regularly these days, although those on fighter squadrons or groups are generally fewer than tomes dealing with the bombers. At the time of writing, most of the 8th Air Force fighter groups have had a history of sorts published, only the elusive 479th having not been covered in recent years. (For more details, see Appendix 2.)

It is quite true that a high number of AAF units put together a record of their recent history immediately after World War 2, but many of these have only a rarity value compared with modern book production. Early post-war paper was of such low quality that photo reproduction was often bad, an aspect generally perpetuated by a handful of modern facsimile reprints. Some do manage to improve the quality a little – but don't expect this always to be the case.

LIBRARIES, BOOK CLUBS AND OTHER SOURCES

Library borrowing can help supplement personal collection of books. In the UK, if the public library should prove unable to supply what is required then there are also the reference libraries such as those of the Imperial War Museum, the RAF Museum and the Air Historic Branch of the Ministry of Defence. While all of these establishments are well worth visiting, research will have to be done on the premises rather than at home – none too convenient for modeling purposes, where ideally the reference should be to hand while construction or painting proceeds.

In the UK, the Public Record Office at Kew and the Documents Section of the IWM and RAF Museum hold a great deal of primary source material on wartime air operations and although the main focus is naturally on the RAF, much USAAF material is available for scrutiny. Such documents will help areas like narrowing down operational flights by individuals and units on given dates, targets and so forth – an example for some of how an interest in model making opens up broader horizons.

Book clubs are another way of obtaining the aviation literature you need. A small saving on the regular cover price (often it must be said eroded by postal charges) makes some titles less of a bargain than they first appear although

taken over a few years of membership, regular orders can offset this drawback by genuine reductions.

A number of relatively new, private book dealers are also helping the individual to build up a useful personal library. Operating a mail order service, most of them regularly publish catalogues of specialist interest. As many references to USAAF aircraft and color schemes are currently out of print, the second-hand dealer is the only source for some of the more rare titles. As most of the dealers state in their catalogs, they welcome lists of "wanted books" required by individual customers. Some will conduct a free search or do this in return for a small fee.

EVENTS AND SHOWS

Many modelers avidly attend the various air events that fill the calendar each year. Air shows present an exciting mix of flying and static warbirds and contemporary aircraft,

ABOVE **A huge range of hard cover and soft cover general reference books are available on the subject of USAAF Fighters.** *Aces and Wingmen* **(2 vols) focuses on USAAF fighter units in Europe.**

Dana Bell's
Aviation Color Primers
IPMS-USA National Convention Special, Virginia Beach, August 2002

No. 1: US Export Colors of WWII

BOTTOM: Hudson Mk.V(SR)s await delivery in New York, spring 1941. Although the original image is stained, the aircraft clearly display their Lockheed-applied Dark Earth, Dark Green, and Sky Grey camouflage. Note the similarly painted Douglas Bostons and uncamouflaged Lockheed Lodestars. (NASM-Arnold Collection)

TOP: A Baltimore Mk.IIIA warms its engines at the snow-covered Martin plant during the winter of 1942/43. US paints match the RAF desert camouflage of Dark Earth, Middle Stone, and Azure Blue. (Martin via Piet)

17 of 200

ABOVE Occasionally, limited edition reference works will be made available. This excellent summary of US export colors of World War 2 was self-published by historian Dana Bell to accompany his seminar at the 2002 IPMS National Convention. The presentation of this stapled book is simple, but the information is outstanding.

trade stands and other attractions. In the UK, venues such as Duxford, Old Warden, Biggin Hill and the Royal International Air Tattoo at Fairford are supported by a large number of book dealers and model kit stockists and the enthusiast is often able to combine half a year's purchasing at various other outlets to obtain all his needs at one or two shows. Numerous bargains in kits, videos, photographs and ephemera are available and if you miss one of the events early in the year, there are usually two or three dozen more later on both here and abroad. The main shows with an air display element are interspersed with smaller events such as jumbles and book fairs, enough to keep the enthusiast away from home for every weekend of the year, or as long as the wallet will bear it.

VIDEOS

Hitherto unseen film records of World War 2 combat continue to appear as commercial videos.

Other footage, taken by pilots and groundcrews who were in the various war zones, is also available. If you're building a video library, the series from AVI entitled *The Great Planes* includes much to interest the modeler. It covers the main USAAF fighter types in some depth, placing the aircraft in a historical context with interesting contemporary footage. Such videos invariably consist of a mixture of monochrome and color film, the latter bringing forth some real eye openers regarding salient details of interiors, landing gear, propellers, and so forth.

Equally good from the detail point of view are copies of wartime instructional films, which include walk-round exterior checks and full flight data. Using a good quality video recorder incorporating a reliable "freeze frame" control, this footage may be paused and studied at leisure. Ongoing computer sophistication means that stills may also be obtained from video as well as the Internet.

Film sources can undoubtedly add to an individual's knowledge of US fighter color schemes during World War 2 because film has a fascinating habit of turning up some anomalies that are not quite as per regulations. A full color image of an aircraft moving across a screen can hardly be challenged as definitive reference.

With all this data coming at us from all sides and in various mediums, surprisingly there are still gaps to be filled, even in connection with something as familiar as the combat markings of USAAF fighter groups operating in the European Theater. Certain units seem to have had less coverage than others for various reasons and the fact that a short piece of film finally confirms something that has been in doubt for decades, is very satisfying. The same goes for the aircraft flown by the top pilots as well as the rank and file – there is nothing quite like seeing their images on moving film.

Finally, there is that relatively recent but increasingly popular addition to the home entertainment suite, the DVD player. This system offers images on disk of the best available quality and significantly superior to videotape. Numerous television programs are put straight onto DVD, enabling the enthusiast modeler to purchase good quality combat footage as soon as it hits the local supplier.

THE "X" FACTOR

And yet with all the data currently available on US fighters, some questions will remain. Most modelers will have experienced the situation in

LEFT Model magazines are another good source of information. Pictured here are *Scale Aircraft Modelling* from the United Kingdom, and *Replic* from France.

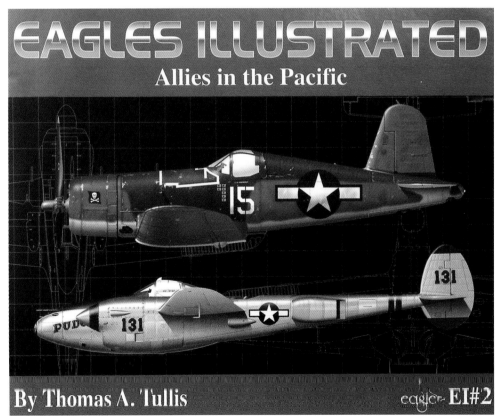

LEFT Some books focus on artwork, such as Tom Tullis' Eagles Illustrated series. Minimal text allows room for many large, attractive profiles. These represent both inspiration and reference for modelers.

RIGHT In addition to Aircraft of the Aces, Osprey Publishing offers several other aviation series.

The Combat Aircraft series details the history, technology and crew of military aircraft. Each book examines a particular aircraft type, and scale drawings and colour profiles illustrate the major variants of each machine

A relatively new addition to Osprey Publishing's list is the Aviation Elite series, which examines the combat histories of fighter and bomber units.

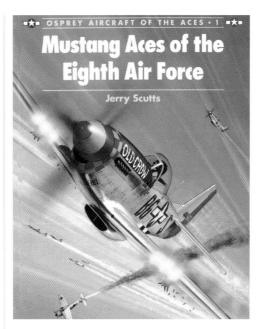

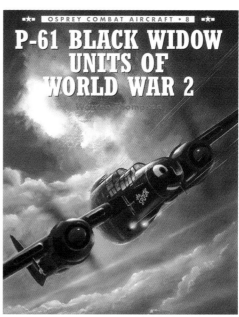

which an attractive color scheme has been noted in a new book or on film. The time, place, unit and even pilot are known, but the final few details important in the finishing of a scale model are still missing. Several wartime US fighter groups dispensed with serial numbers when the fins were overpainted with unit markings; but that doesn't mean that there is no reason to unearth the serial number if only as a clue to the manufacturer's block number and the equipment changes it would have had over the previous one. Serials are the key to variants and technical changes that may be important for a model. Although the majority of fighters did display their AAF identity on the vertical tail, not all the digits are

visible on photographs. So you need it for a model but can't find it – what then?

Fortunately the forward fuselage data block, if readable, will yield those details. But if they can't be discerned, and a similar situation is duplicated a few times over in conjunction with different aircraft types, then it's no wonder that many kits languish. Sadly it is a fact of life that this remaining data may take years to surface as reliable reference. My advice would be to proceed regardless: finish the model in all the markings you can confirm and worry about the missing serial number later. Alternatively, make up a typical serial number for the type in question or add a zero or two in place of missing numbers to remind you.

CHAPTER 3
AVAILABLE PRODUCTS

In this chapter, we'll take a look at the history and development of kits and accessories relating to USAAF modeling, across a variety of scales. With such a wide variety available, a somewhat personal selection inevitably needs to be made – so I premise this with an admission of indulgence for covering some of my personal favorites (as well as the not so favorite!) that have appeared in the previous decades. A list of the most recent releases appears at the end of this chapter for quick reference.

SCOPE AND SCALE

If we count up the number of first-line aircraft types that are covered by the subject matter of this book, we get a baseline five, namely the Bell P-39 Airacobra, Curtiss P-40 Warhawk, Lockheed P-38 Lightning, North American P-51 Mustang and the Republic P-47 Thunderbolt. These were the mainstream fighters that sustained the USAAF's groups and squadrons throughout the war, the Mustang along with the P-61 Black Widow of course

being the latecomers in that they were not ready for US service until 1943 and 1944 respectively.

The enthusiast modeler of today is able to double that figure, assuming the yardstick is kits of aircraft that fired their guns in anger while bearing US markings. By adding the Boeing P-26, Seversky P-35, Curtiss P-36, Douglas P-70, Beaufighter and Spitfire we've already done so. All of those listed above can be built from injection-molded kits, depending on scale. Any that can't are increasingly appearing in the lists of the short-run kit manufacturers.

Further expansion of the list could encompass the Republic P-44 and the P-51H. The first P-82s also flew before the end of the war and if our hypothetical collection is expanded yet again to take in any American originating fighter type that flew between 1939 and 1945, a lengthy list of prototypes may be acquired as models. In a different league to the piston-engine types but still a legitimate model subject is America's first turbojet fighter, the Bell P-59 Airacomet.

Many of the lesser known one-off and prototype contenders for US fighter contracts

LEFT USAAF model kits come in all sizes. Big, 1/24-scale kits of the P-51D Mustang are available from Airfix, Bandai, and more recently Trumpeter of China.

Table 1: list of US Army fighter designations, 1935–45

Type	Manufacturer	Notes	Type	Manufacturer	Notes
CW-21 Demon	Curtiss	production for foreign customers	XP-53	Curtiss	project only
CW-23	Curtiss	production for foreign customers	XP-54 Swoose Goose	Vultee	prototypes only
Y1P-25	Consolidated	project only	XP-55 Ascender	Curtiss	project only
P-26 Peashooter	Boeing	production for USAAC & foreign customers	XP-56 Black Bullet	Northrop	project only
YP-27	Consolidated	project only	XP-57	Tucker	lightweight fighter project
YP-28	Consolidated	project only	XP-58 Chain Lightning	Lockheed	project only
YP-29	Boeing	project only			
P-30	Consolidated	production for USAAC	P-59 Bell	Airacomet	prototype & test series
XP-31 Swift	Curtiss	first monoplane design by company; project only	P-60	Curtiss	project only
P-33	Consolidated	project only	P-61 Black Widow	Northrop	production for USAAF
XP-34	Wedell-Williams	project design for lightweight fighter	XP-62	Curtiss	project only
P-35	Seversky	production for foreign customers	P-63 Kingcobra	Bell	production for foreign customers & USAAF
P-36 Hawk	Curtiss	production for USAAC & foreign customers	P-64	North American	production for foreign customers
YP-37	Curtiss	design forerunner of P-40	XP-65	Grumman	F7F Tigercat forerunner
P-38 Lightning	Lockheed	production for USAAF	P-66 Vanguard	Vultee	production for foreign customers
P-39 Airacobra	Bell	production for USAAF & foreign customers	XP-67 Bat	McDonnell	project only
P-40 Warhawk	Curtiss	production for USAAF & foreign customers	XP-68 Tornado	Vultee	project only
			XP-69	Republic	projection of P-47 design; project only
XP-41	Seversky	project only	P-70	Douglas	adaptation of A-20; production for USAAF
XP-42	Curtiss	project only			
P-43 Lancer	Republic	production for foreign customers	XP-71	Curtiss	project only
P-44 Rocket	Republic	production for foreign customers	XP-72	Republic	projection of P-47; project only
XP-46	Curtiss	project only	XP-75 Eagle	Fisher	prototype design for escort fighter specification
P-47 Thunderbolt	Republic & Curtiss	production for USAAF	XP-77	Bell	lightweight prototype
XP-48	Douglas	project only	XP-78	North American	project only
XP-49	Lockheed	project only based on P-38	XP-79 Flying Ram	Northrop	project only
XP-50	Grumman	Army version of XF5F-1 Skyrocket	XP-80 Shooting Star	Lockheed	prototype for F-80 series
P-51 Mustang	North American	production for RAF & USAAF	XP-81	Convair	project only
XP-52	Bell	project only	P-82 Twin Mustang	North American	production for USAAF/USAF

Note: Some of the missing numbers were never taken up although several were allocated to designs for navy fighters or aircraft in other categories. In this instance "project" can indicate either aircraft actually constructed or a design exercise.

have already been modeled in 1/72 scale and although there may not be kits of all these designs at time of writing, somebody, someday will get around to closing any remaining gaps, and probably quite soon. All that will concentrate the mind of the purist is whether the scale is right, as chances are that more of these fascinating footnotes of aviation history will initially appear in the smaller scales, if only for the fact that anticipated sales will probably be modest and not merit larger investment. Having said that, a glance at recent model journals reveals that manufacturers wishing to inject a little exotica into their lists are certainly not neglecting the larger scales. One can only praise their enterprise in this respect – how many Mustangs will be built in the relatively new scale of 1/18, I wonder?

Just how extensive the US fighter design scene was between the 1930s and the late-1940s can be seen in Table 1 on page 44. Some of the rarer ones would make very impressive kits in 1/48 scale and happily not everything is restricted to the smaller size on the grounds of economy.

MARKINGS MIXING

When it comes to modeling possibilities, foreign aircraft types flying in USAAF markings can extend to the Hurricanes of the Eagle Squadrons (some Sea Hurricane XIIs were also marked with US national insignia for Operation Torch) plus a number of second line types. Famous fighters flying new flags included the P-47Ds of the Brazilian 1° Gruppo, which fought in Italy, the P-47Ds of the Mexican Expeditionary Force in the Pacific, and last but by no means least the P-40B/Cs of the Chinese Nationalist Air Force, alias the Flying Tigers.

Stretching things a little further, the B-25 Mitchell did a turn as a night intruder in the Pacific and CBI so that too could legitimately be included in a representative collection of US Army fighters.

If our list may be lengthened further to include types that did not see combat but were widely used in a Stateside training role, the Bell P-63 Kingcobra can join – as of course can all the first-line types employed not only as trainers but in a host of secondary roles after becoming "War Wearies." These latter fighters can yield a great many off-beat markings schemes, occasionally more exotic than those applied by the front-line squadrons. Needless to say, the Stateside fighter training program was huge and required a constant supply of

surplus P-40Bs, P-47Bs, P-38Fs and P-51As, to mention just a few of the early sub-types.

Fighter training schemes for models were brought to wider public notice by the Japanese Mauve company when it released a 1/48 P-40N in a very bright scheme applied strictly for Zone of the Interior tuition flying as one of the kit's decal options. The painting on the box top even depicted an aircraft in this non-combat scheme, which showed admirable confidence that it was the kit, not the decal sheet, that modelers wanted first and foremost. To read some kit reviews and note the moans aimed entirely at below-par decals, you could be forgiven for thinking that it was actually the other way round!

Wartime US fighters also fulfilled a host of useful but often passive roles as monitor aircraft for heavy bomb groups, weather scouts and general "hacks." Some of these bring into play very unusual markings schemes: for example, you may find a natural metal finish on a long serving example of a given type when 90 percent of its brethren in front-line service were camouflaged. Such unusual schemes, ideal for that different model, still turn up from time to time.

AAF bomber unit histories can be a particularly rich source in respect of unusual fighter schemes. In the ETO, the P-47 tended to predominate in support roles simply because there were so many examples in inventory when the fighter groups generally changed over to the P-51. Best known in this respect are

ABOVE Mustangs must be one of the most kitted model aircraft in history. Tamiya's 1/48-scale P-51B is accurate, beautifully detailed and well engineered. Hasegawa's 1/48-scale P-51D, released some years earlier, is also an excellent kit.

probably the P-47Ds of the 5th Emergency Rescue Squadron, the markings of which have been well documented.

EXOTICA

The years of the late-1990s – early-2000s saw a positive explosion of new kits, many of them from Eastern Europe and the former Soviet Union. These products swelled the kit market to a significant degree, leading to new manufacturers making an impact with kits of aircraft that had rarely been replicated previously. Thus such American fighters as the almost forgotten Vultee P-66 Vanguard and Republic P-43 Lancer, not to mention the one-offs and also-rans, joined the ranks.

Part of the first generation of US monoplane fighters, those mentioned were largely intended for the export market and more familiarly appeared in foreign rather than American colors. In some cases, particularly in China, these deliveries reverted back to US control where they wore that country's national insignia, often for the first time. But whatever the circumstances, if fighters and prototypes of what might be termed the adolescents of an industry still maturing in the early-1940s wore the white star on a blue field, then they may be included in a USAAF model collection. In this way a true chronological history can be created in miniature.

Currently the international kit market makes this possibility much more realistic than it once was. Both the P-66 and P-43 are kitted by Air Collection and Classic Airframe respectively, to 1/48 scale, a model size that rolls on with a burgeoning after-market list of accessories seemingly appearing on a monthly basis. My earlier remarks about the Curtiss forerunners of the P-40 appearing as wartime kits must have been overheard as I note that the US company Joe's Models has now added a YP-37 to its 1/72-scale range.

If the modeler needs to keep pace with everything that is released, subscriptions to a number of journals and periodicals will be *de rigueur*. Titles such as *Scale Aviation Modeler* from the UK and the American Fine Scale *Modeler* are very on the ball, publishing as they do many reviews of kits, decals and products from paint to power tools. The former of these two magazines is specific to aircraft kits while FSM is general with the advantage of carrying small ads for some of the more specialist products from mostly US suppliers. Any one of those advertisements may offer the very item you need to complete a model project, be it a plan, a specially formulated paint, a custom part or a new set of decals.

Arguably the leading journal of its kind in the UK, SAM carries full lists of actual kits, forthcoming releases and fascinating, well-founded rumors of future presentations from all over the world. In any given year the enthusiast modeler will be able to update an ever-changing "wants" list purely from the pages of this one publication. To show what is actually happening in the real world of competition modeling, the editor and staff regularly attend shows to feature the best exhibits. With the advantage of being almost full color throughout, SAM is undoubtedly a good buy.

France and Germany have become leading producers of top quality modeling journals, with the advantage that a slightly different design approach provides the reader with some exceptional photographic spreads of featured full-size aircraft, invaluable to completing models. Among these titles are *Aero Journal*, *Avions*, *Jet & Prop*, *L'Album* and *Replic*. Of course the text is not in English, but then again photographs are international. Should you need these publications but do not wish to incur additional bank charges by personal foreign currency transaction, subscriptions may be placed in the UK through The Aviation Bookshop or Midland Counties Publications, among others.

CLOSING THE GAPS

The widespread availability of American fighter types in kit form has accelerated in recent years. This has significantly extended the possibilities of interesting new color schemes – there has never been a better time to construct a table-top air force. While all the core USAAF types have been kitted at some point in the three decades or so since the hobby of plastic aircraft modeling established itself, a few gaps remain.

Today more kits are covering hitherto lesser-known variants almost to the point where, for example, all the wartime Mustangs from the XP-51 to the P-51H can be built in both the most popular scales. The main question for the modeler is whether the kit is to the scale he or she favors, but I've rarely let that overrule the purchase of a favored type. Provided it's no smaller than 1/72 scale, I go for it. But in terms of scale accuracy it seems to have been inevitable that some aircraft have lent themselves better to the scaling process than others. To paraphrase a well-worn saying, when it comes to plastic aircraft kits, size does seem to matter if it's quality you want.

REPUBLIC
P-47D
THUNDERBOLT

1/48TH SCALE

ACADEMY
HOBBY MODEL KITS

- FULLY ENGRAVED PANEL LINES AND RIVER DETAIL.
- HIGHLY DETAILED COCKPIT INTERIOR AND LANDING GEAR COMPARTMENT.
- OPTIONAL POSITIONED CLEAR CANOPY AND GUN BAY COVERS.
- VARIOUS UNDER WING WEAPONS INCLUDED.

In general the original American quarter scale has historically served this purpose better than any other. The standard was undoubtedly set by Monogram, a company which as long ago as the 1960s produced a range of 1/48-scale kits that left the rest of the industry standing in terms of accuracy. It took years for the manufacturers concentrating on producing kits in 1/72 scale to catch up, which they now have to a degree.

But for years the modeler of this undoubtedly convenient scale had to cut, sand, mix and match almost every part of the airfame to obtain a decent P-51, P-47 or – well, you name it, that accuracy challenge was always present. Quite why this situation prevailed for so long is hard to fathom. Monogram and a few other notable manufacturers surely had no monopoly on their sources of reference to transfer the dimensions of a full-size airplane into a metal mold and ultimately a good plastic construction kit. To show that they could work the trick in sizes other than 1/48 scale too, when these manufacturers occasionally ventured into 1/72 scale they beat the established opposition hollow.

The modeler of today beginning to build kits of American fighters has a significant advantage over his contemporary of, say, 1970. All the mainstream USAAF aircraft can now be built in a variety of scales, particularly if

the vacuformed and multi-media kit is brought into the equation. These latter types of kit play a key role, as some aircraft are not yet obtainable as injection moldings in the larger scales, particularly 1/32 and 1/24. Less robust than injection molded kits, the vacuform process offers the skilled modeler a real challenge as there is much more work under the skin before the final result emerges.

OUT WITH THE OLD?

Many seemingly extinct kits are back on the market, re-released in their original boxes. Whether or not this is a good thing is a matter of opinion; for these kits, if largely unchanged since they were first released, are sharing shelf space with items that are definitely superior in many important respects.

Over the years kits have been obliged, for various reasons, to change their badges and appear "under new management," such as the Japanese Otaki line of 1/48 fighter kits which is currently available from Airfix. There are plenty of other examples. The modern scene can therefore be quite confusing: which kit does the newcomer chose? One answer, apart from reading reviews and keeping files on the details therein is ask members of a group of specialists, who should be able to answer such questions.

ABOVE Academy's P-47D Thunderbolt offers a fairly simple parts breakdown, accurate outline and plenty of ordnance.

Economics have, not surprisingly, governed the plastic kit market since day one. All manufacturers make a substantial investment every time they decide to release a new injection molded kit and for that reason the molds seem to survive even if the parent company goes to the wall. This happened to the well-known UK range of Frog kits when the molds were shipped to Eastern Europe in the days when the Iron Curtain still existed. Despite dire predictions that kits such as the 1/72-scale Curtiss P-40B would never be seen again in the West, the situation rarely occurred. What did happen was that specialist suppliers, still able to obtain rare kits, hiked their prices, sometimes to the point of absurdity, with largely unobtainable (and often very basic) models becoming potential moneyspinners for the few.

Re-release of older kits stabilizes the market and brings prices back to a more realistic level. This is an important consideration if the younger modeler – those the hobby must attract in order to keep it alive and viable – perhaps with limited funds to spare, is to persevere with a pastime that these days has enormous competition from other sectors of the toy and leisure industry.

Not that the modeler of American fighters has really had much cause to complain of any lack of the essential raw materials with which to work. There have always been kits of P-47s, P-38s and P-47s, or so its seems and even if they were once terrible, well, it was that or nothing. You have to go back to the dark ages of plastic modeling in the UK to a point before Airfix released their first 1/72-scale P-51D,

to find little or no choice at all. But by the late-1950s the US modeling scene had got underway with several quite exotic kits, which many UK modelers considered way beyond their means at the time. The line-up included a P-47N and a number of Navy fighters and jet types in 1/48 scale from such manufacturers as Lindberg and Aurora.

Soon other firms including a hard-core group in Japan, added further types and unless the modeler was particularly quick at building and painting, another option had arrived in the local store before the first kit was completed. It was therefore hard to avoid starting a collection of comparable models even if this had not been the original intention.

1/72 SCALE

As the 1/72-scale modelers passed through the seventies and eighties, they saw things gradually improve in terms of the quality of US fighter kits and must have been quite envious at times. More versions of the most famous fighters were also "discovered" by the manufacturers, undoubtedly assisted by regularly published "want" or "wish" lists in the specialist model press.

Things picked up only gradually however; one or two manufacturers even turned the clock back by releasing appallingly inaccurate models, a particularly bad Mustang in 1/72 being recalled by the writer some time after rival firms had got it more or less right. These were also the days when completely new companies appeared, and although they often started their range with the inevitable (and safe) Spitfire, Bf 109 and perhaps a Mustang, we hoped for better; and the subject matter indeed got more ambitious.

Decal companies also began to explore the potential for offering far more comprehensive subjects than the small sheets that accompanied the kit parts packed in a bag or box. This was fine, provided that enough good kits could be purchased to build, for argument's sake, a representative P-51 from each of the Eighth Air Force groups.

In 1972 Lesney Products made a contribution towards the mass production of models by releasing an acceptable P-51D in their Matchbox range. Here was a kit that while only basically detailed had the right outline shape and could be built in some numbers, the result looking well enough to hang decals on.

Latterly the Revell concern, now an amalgam of German, British and American interests with some buying-in of Japanese molds, has released a

BELOW The USAAF used several British aircraft in Europe, including various marks of the Spitfire. ICM offer a Spitfire Mk.VIII with USAAF markings.

LEFT Conversions and detail sets can transform an ordinary plastic kit into a spectacular replica. Little Fokkers produced a P-40B/C nose in resin to convert Hobbycraft's series of P-36 kits to the Tomahawk. The Eduard photo-etched brass set and resin wheels from True Details would also enhance this project.

further range of 1/72-scale fighters, among them a P-40K, P-51B and D and a P-47M. The latter is particularly good and probably the first time that anyone has seen fit to label a late production P-47D update as such. Also, it is only recently that it has been possible to buy a P-40K marketed by a mainstream manufacturer as such in any scale.

"M" FOR FINESSE

Although it was changed considerably under the skin, the P-47M was externally similar to the P-47D-30 and D-40, the Revell kit providing the useful bonus of including a separate fin fillet. Yes, I know we've all hand cut Thunderbolt fin fillets in the past but the section is very thin in this scale and the fairing-in was exacting and took considerable time and effort. Now, as with numerous other examples of P-47 kits, the manufacturers have removed that chore. But to return to an earlier theme, how long has it taken to market a decent "bubbletop" P-47 in this scale?

The Revell P-47M is not the only useful Thunderbolt in the popular smaller scale to hit the shelves, as Hasegawa put out two versions (razorback and bubbletop) in the seventies, both of which were praised in their day. I always felt they were a shade under sized, lacking the chunkiness that one always associates with the T-bolt. This was particularly true if compared to the old Frog razorback.

To bring things up to date, Hasegawa has recently released a second P-47D razorback, which from all accounts appears to be a suitable replacement for the earlier kit that is no longer generally available. The smaller scale end of the market now looks healthier in terms of US fighter subjects than it ever was.

Lesney/Matchbox had a stab at a razorback T-bolt and at least achieved an excellent rear fuselage profile, accurate enough for the inspired modeler to cross kit this with some parts from others to produce a good representation of Republic's mighty machine.

1/48 SCALE

Moving up a scale, the picture vis-à-vis accuracy of outline is and was, much more satisfying. From the day in 1967 that Monogram released their superior P-47D-25 bubbletop complete with cylindrical and "flat" drop tanks, bombs and M-10 rocket launcher tubes, the art of the plastic kit took another upturn. In this scale a new Monogram release rarely disappointed. Bold enough to invest serious money in ever-larger kits in 1/48 scale, this US concern delighted the modeling world with ever more desirable, popular – and some quite esoteric – kit subjects.

When the P-61 came out in 1974, the standard of kit tooling took another giant leap

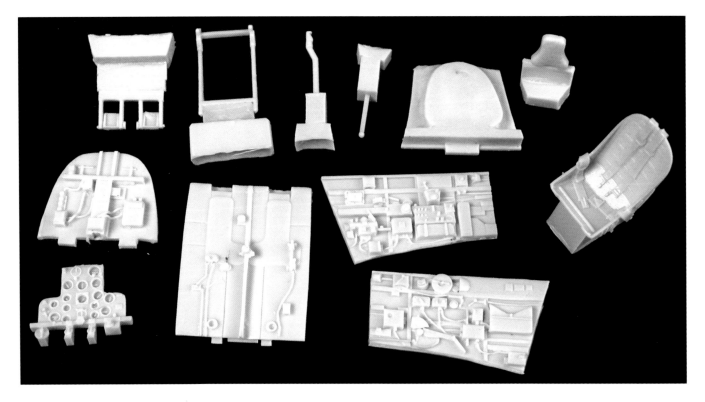

ABOVE Cutting Edge's resin replacement cockpit for the P-40B/C seen in close-up. Today's generation of cockpit sets feature exquisite detail, and they are available for a wide range of USAAF fighter aircraft. Brands such as Cutting Edge, Black Box, Aires and CMK maintain a very high standard of detail.

forward. It beat the previous best of this aircraft in the larger scale, that from Aurora, a company that was certainly a plastic-kit pioneer but unfortunately lacked the design expertise to be found at Morton Grove, Illinois. No other US manufacturer seemed quite able to equal Monogram's prolific program of new 1/48-scale releases, which spanned some 30 years. There were subjects that the company did not get around to while it remained independent. Sold to Mattel before being absorbed by Revell, the expertise of its designers now appears under a different label. The important thing is that the quality of the kits has not slipped.

Not that the name on the box really matters as long as the contents are accurate, well molded and, hopefully, depicting a variant that has not previously appeared. Huge duplication of kit subjects (many, it must be said, being of US fighters) must have had a detrimental effect on the sales figures of some companies, particularly if the kits they produced appeared to be over-priced. As a rule though the picture has been positive even if the build up of different aircraft types, and the filling in of long standing gaps (such as an accurate P-47B), has been slow.

Over the years the Japanese brand leaders, particularly Hasegawa and Tamiya, have mastered the art of releasing types that fit neatly into what was a Monogram-dominated scale but without too much duplication. Tamiya's 1997 release of a Beaufighter is a case in point: finished in American markings it

makes an interesting comparison with the P-61. Recently the USAAF night fighter trio has been completed by Academy's P-38M, a variation on their existing P-38J/L kits in 1/48 scale.

AMERICAN SPITS

Also very important to the AAF order of battle was the Spitfire in various marks, mainly the II, V, VII, IX and XI, the latter a photographic reconnaissance variant that did sterling work. The Spitfire kit picture in 1/48 scale was not too rosy for many years: Monogram was the first to put out a Mk IX that was not quite the company's best effort, although again the inclusion of a cylindrical belly tank showed just how careful the company was in its research. Then Otaki added their very acceptable Mk VII, Airfix followed with a Mk V and before too long we all got some reliable printed details on Supermarine fighters marked with "stars and bars." These revealed that there were many more American Spitfires than we'd ever imagined. During the 1990s, four more companies released 1/48-scale Spitfires. These comprised Hasegawa, with several variations on the Mk V, Mk VIII and Mk IX; Tamiya, with a Mk I and a few Mk Vs; Ocidental, with a Mk IX and Mk XVI; and ICM, with Mks VII, VIII, IX and XVI.

EARLY NIGHT FIGHTER

Finally, there was the P-70. An excellent 1/48-scale Douglas Havoc from AMT-ERTL broke new ground and although being a later A-20G variant with a rear turret the kit can be converted back to produce a P 70A with "open" rear gun position, as used in combat in the Pacific during 1942-43. This injection molded kit followed in the wake of a superb vacuform A-20G/J from Koster Aviation Enterprises that was equally adaptable to a P-70.

While the 1/48-scale Thunderbolt situation remained much the same as it used to be in 1/72 by being dominated by variations of the early or late P-47D, in 1995 Academy-Minicraft released an excellent P-47N followed by another from Revell-Monogram/PRO-Modeler shortly afterwards, thus doubly filling another gap. Long gone was the Aurora 1/48 scale P-47N which the author recalls laboriously turning into – well, a P-47N. I still have the prop, and wonder what ever happened to the rest of it.

Hasegawa meanwhile had produced the all but definitive late P-47D-30 model complete with the dorsal fin strake. This was followed even more recently by a razorback D which, compared to the still very acceptable Monogram kits, had fine engraved panel lines, items such as optional flattened tires for a typically loaded down fighter bomber, plus a full range of ordnance. Tamiya's 1/48-scale P-47 Razorback released in 2002 signaled yet another step up the quality ladder, with beautiful surface texture, excellent details and many optionsincluding bombs, drop tanks, rockets, three alternate propeller styles and dropped flaps.

Regarding the underwing munitions, one has only to collect a small number of kits to quickly accumulate a full US ordnance depot's-worth of aerial weaponry in plastic form, almost everything being available in increasingly near to scale dimensions. One area the manufacturers have thus far shied away from has been to release any parachute fragmentation bombs. Hung on fighter wing racks or garlanded around a 500 lb bomb, the small but deadly "parafrags" were widely used and it is to be hoped that one of the cottage industry suppliers is even now working on a set that may be adapted to several fighter kits, as well as bombers. Even in one of the larger scales parafrags would be very small, with tiny fins and attachment lugs – but they would certainly be a useful addition to a plastic arsenal.

Ordnance has indeed come a long way since the pioneering days of plastic modeling. USAAF drop tanks, ferry tanks, bombs and rockets either in triple M-10 tubes or the high velocity type suspended from zero-length launchers, constituted by far the most numerous add-ons

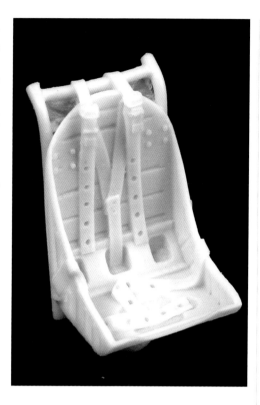

for the wartime US fighter bomber, irrespective of type. In the more exotic category were the 20mm cannon suspended from the wing racks of some 8th Air Force P-47s. In passing, I'd suggest that this arrangement would make a very interesting model subject.

ROCKETS

More US fighters were fitted to use high velocity aircraft rockets (HVARs) than is perhaps generally realized. The P-40N was adapted to carry the M-10s and some aircraft were fitted with them for operations in China. Alternatively, six HVARs per wing on zero-length launchers, as tantalizingly indicated on several breaker's yard photographs taken after the end of the war, was an alternative. This was I believe, a very late production addition to the P-40 and one possibly restricted to US-based examples for training purposes. No good photos of P-40s carrying a full compliment of HVARs seem to have surfaced as yet but time will undoubtedly turn up confirmation.

HVAR rocket launchers can also be added to the P-61 while the P-38 carried the M-10 triple tubes attached to the fuselage pod. Numerous photos exist of Lightnings testing "trees" of HVARs in the US and recent literature indicates that these were fitted to first-line aircraft in the Pacific, mainly in the immediate postwar era when AAF groups undertook occupation duty in Japan.

The P-47Ns operating in the Central Pacific also carried the M-10 launcher to some extent, although the later model Thunderbolts were more commonly fitted with zero-length launchers. Some of these rockets had shaped-charge heads, which were not unique to the theater as they were also seen on operational Thunderbolts in Europe.

LARGER STILL: 1/32 SCALE

In terms of the number of available kits in each of the most popular scales, the selection gradually dwindles the larger you go. Models in 1/32 scale offer quite a challenge but with exciting possibilities for a very dramatic end product. Limited in subject matter and showing considerable variation in quality, this scale seems to be relatively low in popularity, probably because of the work involved in rectifying faults. So few are the injection-molded kits in this scale that lend themselves to US Army markings that a list (subject to some current updating) of well established kits

BELOW The subtle profiles of propeller blades are sometimes lost on model manufacturers. Ultracast also produce accurate propeller blades. These are Curtiss Standard Cuffed 4-Blade Propellers, designed for Tamiya's P-51 kits.

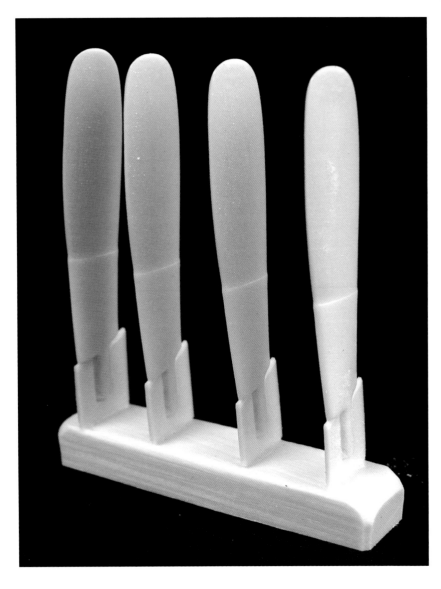

is quite short: P-38 (2); P-40B (2); P-40E (1); P-47D (2); P-51B (2); P-51D (4); and Spitfire (2). Even the P-38 entry, the Revell kit, should be qualified as being a basic P-38J and an alternative "droop snoot" version using the same molds but including the necessary clear nose section used by a navigator/bombardier. The P-40B total includes one conversion and a full multi-media kit.

One of the later Mustangs and one Spitfire V, both by Hasegawa, are excellent while the Revell P-40E is a potential competition winner provided that a fair amount of work is carried out. The same cannot be said for the two Revell P-47s and the P-51B, at least not as they come from the box. Things are however improving in this respect and Craftworks of the US has recently released a 1/32-scale P 51B. Resin model manufacturer J. Rutman has also recently released 1/32-scale kits of the P-51B Mustang, plus Razorback and Bubbletop versions of the P-47. These kits are very accurate and well detailed.

The other Spitfire V is another Revell kit which was superseded by the later Hasegawa offering. This superb kit is appropriate for conversion to an early Eagle Squadron example of a Mk Vc, as widely used by US units in the Mediterranean.

The Mustang listing rounds off with the two early Monogram kits of the P/F-51D which were released both as a standard kit and the so-called "Phantom Mustang," which had a completely transparent airframe designed to show the essential internal details inside the fuselage and wings. It came complete with a control plinth that retracted the wheels via a battery-operated lever and also released the wing bombs.

If that kind of activity does nothing for you, it is fortunate that either of the 1/32-scale Monogram kits may be adapted to improve the Revell P-51B, principally by enabling it to borrow a nose section that suggests that a Packard-Merlin is inside rather than something with much more modest power output as indicated by the slim nose of the P-51B out of the box. The chopping and changing process does work and the result shows a spectacular improvement in outline.

Many other areas of the Revell kit need changing or modifying but an acceptable model can be made, particularly if the kit's optional Malcom hood is chosen. This will at least reduce the number of heavy hinges cut into the opening sections of the six-piece canopy in order to provide operating features. These are otherwise acceptably thin and another example of "spoiling

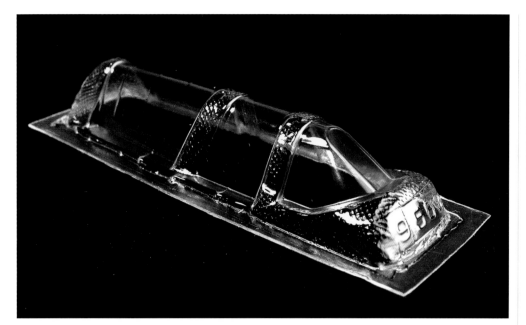

the ship" for want of a little more care. But the real answer is to have a completely new canopy – of either type – modeled separately. As noted earlier a new kit of the P-51B in 1/32 scale has been announced and hopefully, it will render all this hacking up of other kits unnecessary.

Incidentally, Revell later re-tooled their 1/32-scale P-51B into a P-51D. Although I've never seen the kit, it was apparently updated only in regard to the obvious canopy and fuselage changes, the many other errors being perpetuated – clearly an opportunity wasted.

Revell's option of a razorback Thunderbolt has some exciting possibilities in this scale – but again the company nearly ruined a potentially fine kit by cutting corners on some important details. When the earlier kit was joined by a P-47D-25 bubbletop, it was disappointing in that the designer had miscalculated the shape of the canopy. It lacks the characteristic high point of the hood aft of the windscreen section, making it impossible to use unless a replacement can be molded.

THE P-38 LIGHTNING

Revell also gave the modeling world the sole P-38 in this scale. Like its single-engine contemporaries, the overall size is impressive and with work, the fighter can be made to look particularly convincing. Locomotive style rivets cover the entire airframe in the majority of these kits, the Lightning being no exception and a substantial amount of smoothing down is necessary prior to assembly. But with a basically good outline shape, the big Lightning goes together well enough, with the prospect of adding a considerable amount of detail to bring it up to competition-winning standard.

With such work carried out it could stand with the P-40E as one of the best two kits in 1/32 scale by Revell, as no major airframe modifications are called for. The Warhawk and others in this series are re-released by the company from time to time, so you won't necessarily have to pay collectors' prices for them.

Otherwise most of these older 1/32-scale kits can still be found in specialist outlets: astute modelers, realizing that these were quite long term building projects, invested in a suite of drop tanks which were released as vacuform sets by US manufacturers while the kits were still relatively new. Thus the P-38 and the other US fighters in the series could have their distinctive additional fuel tanks, few of which actually were provided in the kits at least on their first-run release. Later kits did include tanks, however.

The 1/32-scale Revell P-38, P-40 and P-47 all contain removable panels to expose areas of the engine, which can of course, be detailed over and above what the instruction sheet recommends. Although the P-38 kit only includes one Allison, there are enough model engines in this scale to add the other one and detail both if required. With both power plants *in situ* and more panels removed this could be a challenging project. Displaying each engine separately adjacent to the model itself is an alternative. In any event, some work certainly needs to be done in regard to engine panels on these large-scale kits, as those on both the P-38 and P-47 were seemingly afterthoughts with a poor fit.

Finally, a 1/32-scale Revell Beaufighter could be completed as a USAAF night fighter.

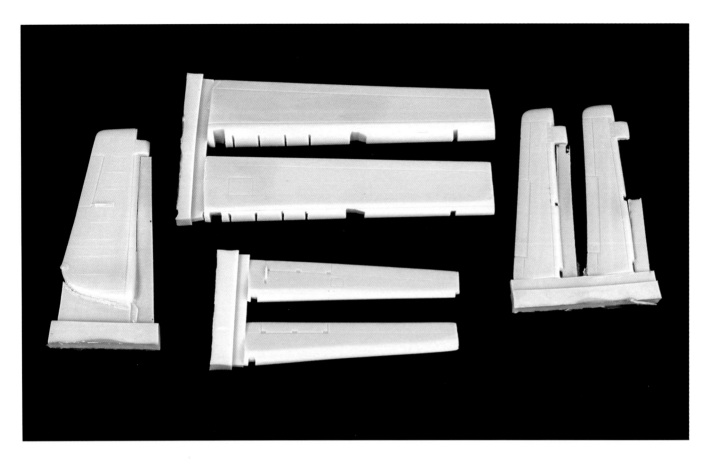

ABOVE Separate control surfaces are helpful when depicting deflected ailerons and rudder, or dropped flaps and elevators.

USAAF "Beaus" carried the standard variety of artwork and names as applied to other types and there is a choice of variants.

THE GIANTS: 1/24 SCALE

At 1/24 scale there are three P-51Ds, by Airfix, Bandai, and more recently Trumpeter. None unfortunately is without its flaws, but dedicated work and a degree of cross-kitting should bring about an extra special model that is undeniably impressive. Airfix again miscalculated the nose contours and repeated the same error for a second time on a 1/72-scale P-51D. The profile of the Trumpeter P-51 kit nose is also poor: this new kit has other shape deficiencies too. But the sheer size of a Mustang in this scale is inspirational, ideal for the really long term projects that can incorporate a massive amount of scratch-built detail, perhaps incorporating brass etch and/or resin components.

Whether or not you model figures to go with kits, the 1/24-scale Mustangs also inspire the keen modeler to incorporate the pilot. Being large enough to be of recognizable human proportions, he might look good leaning on the wing or posed getting into or out of the cockpit, perhaps clutching a handful of maps or holding up five fingers in time honored fashion to signify the achievement of "ace in a day" status. Many model figures appear a little squashed and rather

wooden but the larger size enables limbs to be reset so that your own composition may be arranged.

All three of these large-scale kits vary considerably in detail and design approach. While Bandai opted for a smoother surface with acceptable scribed panel lines (including optional transparent covers over the gun breeches to show the detail) Airfix went overboard with countersunk rivets which were a little over scale. Numerous coats of paint will reduce the effect of these but the kit's outline errors incline the modeler more towards the Japanese product. The latter shows a varied approach in that it has zero-length rocket launchers molded into the wing undersides. Airfix also provide HVARs, but with separate launchers. The Trumpeter kit features relatively restrained surface texture compared to its 1/24-scale counterparts, and a generally high level of detailing. However, specific items including the cockpit and the machine gun leading edge fairings still need plenty of extra work.

Each kit contains parts to build up the engine, the result of which is, not surprisingly, a substantial sub-assembly in its own right. By splitting the servicing access panels in a similar way to the real thing, Airfix make it relatively difficult to leave the engine out, should this be preferred to save time. Displaying the Merlin engine as a separate subject alongside the aircraft will interest those who wish to add super detail to it, although the Bandai product presents a simpler kit that may be built without incorporating the engine block, giving the modeler more of a choice.

Bandai also included a pair of transparent gun bay covers through which the Brownings and their belts may be viewed. One of several similar approaches by kit manufacturers, this idea never really took off.

The most recent US Fighter addition the these giants is Trumpeter's Spitfire Mk Vb. This impressive kit is well detailed and quite accurate in outline. In fact, it is possibly the best kit released in 1/24 scale to date. Airfix has also modified its old large-scale Spitfire Mk I to Mk Vb standards, including options of Vokes filter, Aboukir filter, clipped wingtips, Rotol or De Havilland propeller assemblies and alternate canopies. However, the impressive tally of extras does not compensate for the difference in overall tooling quality between the Airfix kit and the much better Trumpeter offering.

SOLE REPRESENTATIVES – SO FAR

As far as USAAF subjects were concerned in 1/24 scale, that was that. No P-47, no P-40, no anything else that could readily carry white stars, outside of a major conversion of the Airfix Mk I Spitfire to a later variant to create a USAAF operated machine. We wait, probably in vain, for a P-47 to appear as a complete injection-molded kit in 1/24 scale from one of the mainstream suppliers. Even the vacuform kit manufacturers largely shy away from such substantial investments in plastic: several 1/32-scale fighters have been released but the writer knows of no readily available additions in 1/24 scale at time of writing.

However, the old adage tells us that if you wait long enough, it happens. Current ventures into several shorter run, multi-media kits to a very large scale may well bring about more big USAAF fighters. It would be good to be able to put a 1/24-scale P-47, P-39 or P-40 on the competition table in future years, so here's hoping.

SOURCES OF SUPPLY

The keen modeler can do no better than to buy through one of the mail order specialists. These can take the hassle out of buying direct, and unless there is a particularly good hobby shop in your town, supply of new releases can be patchy at best. Shops usually order small quantities of kits at a time, there usually being

a restriction on shelf space; they sell the first batch, then wait for the distributor to restock them. If there is any problem at the shipper's end, you could end up waiting months.

Alternatively an account taken out with any reputable mail order specialist, should ensure that specific requirements are catered for with the minimum of delay. As always, much depends on whether or not the kit is home grown. If it is imported, this certainly has a bearing on the speed of delivery to local outlets. Fortunately the larger companies use a network of agents who also distribute the kits within various countries.

To emphasize the ongoing popularity of kits of US fighters, the list that appears on page 56 covers some of the models released or announced in the last five years or so. Not all are new, as the current scene includes numerous re-issues with new decals and maybe new parts, plus changes of manufacturer wherein molds are either transferred or kits are bought in and marketed by firms under a different name from that of the original. As can be seen, the appearance of a hitherto rare type in kit form seems to spawn a spate of imitators – there are no less than three 1/48-scale Vultee P-66s in this list.

BELOW Many different engines, both radial and in-line, are available. Probably the most prolific supplier of these resin power plants is a company called Engines and Things. The quality of detail and casting does not match the best after-market items of today, but they do represent a sound basis for an accurate engine.

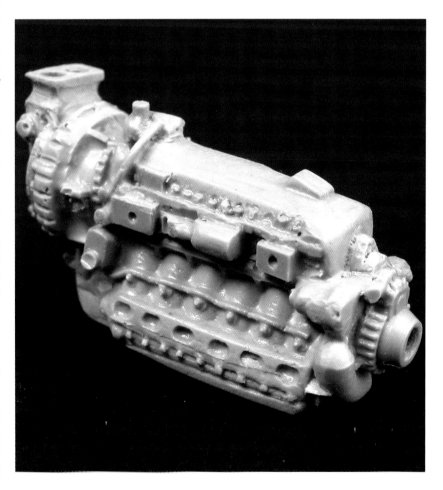

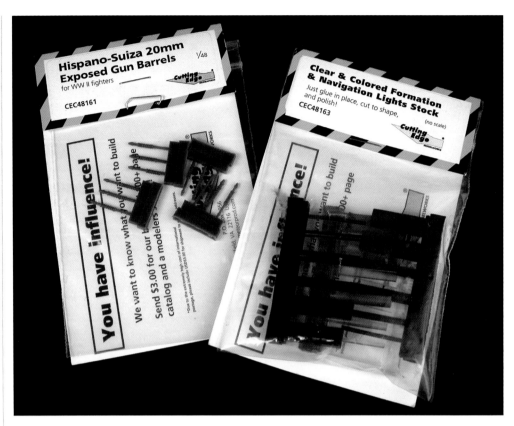

Manufacturer	Aircraft type	Manufacturer	Aircraft type
1/72 scale		ICM	Spitfire Mks VII/IX
Academy	P-40	ICM	P-51B/C
LF Models	TP-40N	ICM	P-51D
Hasegawa	Bristol Beaufighter	Pend Oreille Model Kits	Vultee P-66
Academy	P-51B/C	*1/32 scale*	
High Planes Models	Douglas DB-7A	Revell	P-40E
InTech	P-51B	Combat Models	Spitfire Mk IX
Italeri	Spitfire Mk Vb	Craftworks	P-51B
MPM	P-40F/L	Trumpeter	P-51D
MPM	P-47N	*1/18 scale*	
Wingnut International	Republic XP-72	MPM/HML	P-51D
Planet Models	Vultee XP-54		
	Swoose Goose		
RS Models	XP-38		
RS Models	Hawk 75		
1/48 scale			
Accurate Miniatures	Beaufighter (various marks)		
Eduard	P-39Q/P-400		
Hasegawa	P-47D		
Historic Plastic Models	P-51H		
Minicraft	P-38J		
Ocidental Models	Spitfire Mk IX		
Modelcraft	Spitfire Mks VII/IX		
POMK	Vultee P-66		
S Models	Vultee P-66		
SMER	P-51A		
Tamiya	P-47D Razorback		
Fonderie Miniature	P-63A Kingcobra		
Hobbycraft	YP-59/P-59A Airacomet		

CHAPTER 4
BASIC CONSTRUCTION

How basic is "basic'? It must vary depending on the age and skill level of the individual modeler, the range of tools her or she is able to use with confidence, the time available to devote to modeling and numerous other factors. The detail some individuals manage to cram into the smaller scale kits shows truly outstanding skill. To those who consistently win prizes for their work, the rest of us can have nothing but the utmost admiration.

Most modern injection-molded plastic kits provide a straightforward step by step guide to building each sub-assembly. If there is a choice of variants the alternate parts are clearly labeled. That said, it is useful to run an eye over the salient design points of the different aircraft under review. The bulk of this chapter will therefore describe various primary-type kits (the Lightning, Thunderbolt, Mustang and so on) following some of the general assembly steps which, with obvious variations, are similar for all injection-molded plastic kits.

PRIMARY TYPES

The general shape of the American wartime fighter is of course very familiar to those that have studied even the most basic reference and it goes without saying that the miniaturized version should have all the major parts duplicated accurately. With due regard to certain limitations of the molding process and the relatively small size of most plastic kit parts, kit design may result in a different breakdown of parts but the end result of assembling kit A from manufacturer Y should end up looking much like that of kit B from manufacturer Z.

In the real world there is more variation than one would expect but much depends on the scale, the age of the molding and in essence, something one might well call "tradition." This latter factor means that a range of kits from the same manufacturer will usually have one-piece horizontal tailplanes with location slots whereas a kit from a rival range may

LEFT A 1/48-scale Bell P-39D Airacobra, modeled by Brett Green. You do not always need to build a new model in order to have a new USAAF fighter aircraft in your collection. With some care and planning, it is possible to obtain good results by refurbishing an old model – a process that we will demonstrate in the photographs that appear in this chapter. This model is Eduard's excellent 1/48-scale P-400 kit that was originally built as an Australian P-39. Thanks to the refurbishment process, it is now wearing a new identity.

RIGHT This shows the kit as originally built, an Australian P-39. Although initial construction was free of major problems, a couple of basic shortcomings of this model were not addressed the first time around. These were the thick trailing edges and the tricky fit of the characteristic "car doors." The first issue was ignored. The second issue was initially avoided by depicting both doors open. Reconditioning commenced with the removal of detail parts. Fortunately, parts including the undercarriage legs, gear doors and car doors were secured with Superglue. Superglue provides a strong join, but it does not actually weld plastic parts together in the same way as polystyrene cement. Firm pressure is often sufficient to break the brittle bond without serious damage. Small details were stored in a ziplock plastic bag to ensure they were not lost. The next task was the removal of decals. First, brown packing tape was applied over the top of the decals, then ripped off. This method is usually very effective at removing decals, but these markings proved more stubborn. Even the generous application of decal softening solution made no difference. There was no choice other than to sand off the markings, first with a sanding stick followed by progressively finer abrasive paper.

invariably break the tailplanes down into six separate sections (top and bottom solid section plus a pair of elevators) and perhaps also provide a pin which passes through the fuselage to support the elevators.

This in turn is the result of the same design team opting for a similar approach no matter what the subject may be. For the modeler this approach is a mixed blessing. It may add up to increased building time, especially if the solid tailplane, as per our example, ends up looking exactly the same as the more complex one once the latter has been assembled. It is an unfortunate fact of modeling life that extra sub-assemblies do not always guarantee that, for example, trailing edges of flying surfaces end up as thin as they should be.

Another factor is the highly acceptable increase in larger alternate parts such as nose and tail sections. These are either included in the kits as standard injection-molded parts or as solid resin sections which are designed to butt joint an appropriately truncated fuselage in the case, say, of a new nose. Such a large new section obviously requires careful alignment and use of an effective adhesive, because in the main resin is a good deal denser than plastic and therefore heavier.

TRAILING EDGES & JOINT LINES

In regard to building an alternative version of a kit, I surely cannot be alone in having made the understandable error in cementing together two parts of a new vertical tailplane and finding an annoying joint line or step has to be sanded away. Understandable? Well, this poor result is often only because the instruction sheet has been followed to the letter: what one should do is to make the necessary cuts to remove the existing tailplane and attach the male and female halves separately, before cementing the fuselage as a complete half in the usual way. This I find minimizes the risk of creating a stepped joint, one that can be surprisingly difficult to remove once the fuselage halves are together. Once dry, the inside face of the fuselage half, the edge that takes the adhesive, can be sanded down. This is important as the alternate part may be slightly deeper than the fuselage.

The general advice here should be that in some kits, the separate parts provided for an alternate version can be slightly larger or smaller than the main fuselage moldings, or so it seems. The difference can hardly be measured but it will be revealed the minute the adhesive dries, so always be alert to the risk of a bad fit. Otherwise, you'll invariably find out about it at an advanced stage of construction. It is doubly irksome to have to sand down more than usual or in extremis to have to prize a sub-assembly apart to re-align a bad joint.

Remedial work is of course a possibility, as we can see from the accompanying images of the P-39 reconditioning, but in modeling, as in many other aspects of life, prevention is better than cure.

OTHER TROUBLE

Years of lying dormant at varying temperatures can have a detrimental effect on older kits, the parts of which appeared to be a perfect fit when it was purchased.

Some components do not age well at all. Unbeknown to me the "real rubber" PVC tires issued in the Airfix 1/24-scale P-51D lost their flexibility over the years and have almost molded themselves solid to the wheel hubs. This and other large kits do not always offer a plastic alternative, so if the rubber boots have perished, finding replacements might be difficult. If you have these kits in the loft it may be worth checking on the state of their tires.

CORRECTING A P-47

Differing design methods of achieving the same end may frustrate the modeler who likes to cross-kit to obtain a good result by utilizing the best features of several. Let's assume that a 1/72-scale P-47 is being made: there will be two methods of mating the wings to the fuselage – butt-jointed, or as a one-piece lower section which incorporates part of the lower fuselage, the object presumably being to obtain the correct dihedral angle and a more accurate lower fuselage line when viewed in profile. This does not always happen, of course because model kit manufacturers are only as good as their reference sources and occasionally end up as confused as the rest of us. Don't assume that they necessarily have much more comprehensive

references than you do, as the results sometimes refute this.

A few examples will emphasize the problem. The Lesney Matchbox P-47 in 1/72 scale has a razorback profile that makes it a desirable kit to tackle although a glance at the contents of the box almost makes one wince. The kit sprues were originally colored a bright powder blue and navy blue – hardly an inspirational choice, but typical of most of this company's early products. Two-tone plastic was different to the way most other kits were sold and the marketing men appeared to have believed that this approach was a winner.

This particular P-47 has some redeeming features but others that are not so. Although the airframe outline aft of the engine firewall is acceptable, there is much reservation on the vague way the cowling flaps are presented. The cowling itself seems to fall into one of two categories used by manufacturers of 1/72-scale Thunderbolts – too slim or too fat.

The Matchbox kit errs in the former category, which is marginally harder to correct. But assuming that an alternative cowling is not to hand, the flaps need to be removed and replaced by a correctly scribed, thin strip of Plasticard or a set cut from another kit. Other fuselage details need attending to at the same time, particularly the ventral intakes and exhausts associated with the function of the supercharger, plus the waste gates in each side of the fuselage. As molded, all these details are too small. The distinctive turboblower intakes and exhaust doors in the lower front fuselage also need improving before the next stage in construction is reached. One option is to smooth down the entire fuselage at the same time as re-scribing the cowl flaps. Sets of Airfix and Frog P-47 kit wings can be made to fit without too much filling. Fortunately, the Matchbox kit, in common with many other Thunderbolt models, has straightforward butt joint top and bottom wing sections. Be warned though, the sheer time taken to convert one 1/72-scale P-47 into what it is supposed to be in the first place is disproportionately too high at times.

The building up of one or more spares boxes can prove invaluable in any conversion work with 1/72-scale plastic kits. "Building up" is a rather misleading statement, as spare parts tend to accumulate rapidly seemingly without much help from the modeler. The source may be unused extra parts supplied with kits to build alternative versions or, as is so often the case with military aircraft, large amounts of ordnance. Everything is worth keeping for future use although I have to admit that after a few years you have more spares than you'll ever be able to use. In something of a "Catch-22" situation, as kits improve, so the need for doing your own customizing tends to lessen but spares still accumulate because multiple examples of the same kit will of course keep yielding an almost equal number of spare items.

MUSTANGS IN DETAIL

A long term favorite with modelers, the North American Mustang line began in model terms with the later production version, the P-51D. Rarely did any other variant see the light of day for years and those that did were less than worth the effort. The breakthrough came when Accurate Miniatures released their first four kits some years ago. The Allison-engine examples were followed with the recent P-51B/C kits, AM climbing the P-51 variant ladder from the right direction, so to speak.

In the larger scales the Mustang fared quite well, the American and Japanese model companies adding it to their respective lists on a regular basis. Hawk created something of milestone with a P-51D in 1/48 scale, which first appeared in 1962. For years this was the yardstick against which other Mustang kits were judged and there was an interesting rider to its appearance. IPMS USA's *Quarterly Journal* ran a review, complete with a list of items necessary to detail the kit, plus some Technical Order manual drawings of the cockpit interior. Unfortunately these were in error insofar as the manuals were for an F-51D rather than the wartime model. The upshot was that model Mustangs began to appear with radio aerial wires stretching from the canopy to the fin. These were not actually needed on World War 2 Mustangs but few people appeared to know this including model

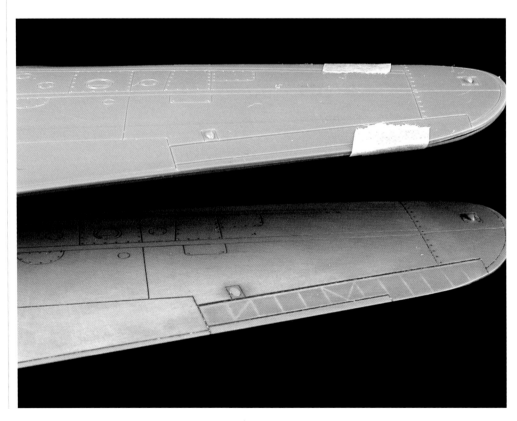

RIGHT The magnitude of the problem with the trailing edges can be seen in this photo. The top view shows the thick, unmodified trailing edge, and the bottom view is the wing after thinning. This will be very noticeable on the finished model.

manufacturers, who started to market kits with a tiny hole in the canopy to take the wire.

Later kits, such as that by Fujimi were not really superior, despite in this case, a full set of moveable control surfaces (the Hawk model had none) including flaps, engine detail and so forth. Separate flaps were quite unusual items to find in any plastic kit at that time, which is rather odd, as moveable ailerons (rather pointless items for an aircraft on the ground) have long been staple items in kits. The pity of it was that the rest of this particular Fujimi kit suffered from some obvious outline errors that tended to put modelers off.

Tamiya's subsequent release of a much superior P-51D was followed by a P-51B in this scale, another example of manufacturers, ever mindful of the competition, filling up gaps in their own list. Pity the poor modeler, who may not, for various reasons, wish to automatically purchase all the Mustangs and Thunderbolts in a given scale as they appear, trying to sort out which is the current best. In a world where today's hit is tomorrow's second place kit, he must be confused at times. Added to that is the fact that the after-market firms always seem to go one better than even the most highly praised kit by releasing corrected parts even before you've even acquired the kit and noticed it to be even slightly below par.

The only answer is to read as many reviews of the new arrival as possible and try to arrive at a personal judgment; we've all seen the model magazine article that praises a kit beyond compare yet prints an accompanying photo that can contradict this.

GETTING INTO THE P-51

Understandably one of the most popular of model kits subjects, the superlative P-51 Mustang in all its guises was a war winner in every sense of the phrase. From its British inspired origins to occupation duty in a defeated Germany and Japan, Mustangs flew thousands of sorties to speed Allied victory. Along the way they were painted in a dazzling array of color schemes and personal markings, enough to keep the enthusiast modeler in work for as many years as the P-51 remained operational. That time span would of course take in the colors of numerous air forces other than the US but the units equipped with it during World War 2 have given us hundreds of markings schemes; so many that a modeler could happily spend his entire time making only models of the P-51 if that were his choice.

For years the only injection-molded plastic kits available represented the revised, bubble canopy P-51D of late-1943, six variants or so into North American's eventual production cycle of some 15,000 examples. But now, the whole range of the aircraft that originated with the NA 73X of 1940 may be built in model form.

DETAILS

Mustang floors were simple wooden boards, as you can readily tell by the heavy grain effect

RIGHT The remainder of the paint was removed with thinners and a clean rag. I wanted to show off the cockpit detail on one side of the aircraft, but retain the clean lines of the fuselage on the other side while retaining a view of the nice interior. The windows in the doors of the P-39 rolled down like those in a car. I sliced off the top of the port side door (the section containing the window), drilled holes in the window around the inside of the frames, then used a sharp hobby knife to cut out the "glass." The empty frame was glued onto the canopy, then the door itself was test-fitted. Some trimming was required to achieve a flush fit.

some kits have on this component part. It would be a very coarse piece of wood indeed that still showed the slightest trace of grain even in 1/24 scale, so all the modeler needs to do is to paint it an appropriate color and add a little discoloration in the form of faded or darkened patches.

Many operational P-51s had the mechanism at the lower end of the control column protected by a canvas or leather boot, which is usually represented in kits. This is painted in an appropriate shade of dark brown to represent leather or lighter brown to indicate fabric – although I am the first to admit I have no idea if and when the different materials were used. My guess is that earlier aircraft used leather but as production built up, a cost saving was made on the use of this material, and a cheaper fabric was then used.

A warbird or any good close-up photograph will reveal salient points about the P-51 which might need slimming down for greater scale accuracy. These include the central rod in the belly air intake; the "solid" or perforated engine breather plate on each side of the lower nose; braces for the tailwheel doors (plus an oleo dust boot); formation light lenses and the curved, perforated canopy brace in the rear cockpit behind the pilot's head.

One item that no Mustang kit I know of includes is the admittedly tiny aerials on the fin for the AN/APS-13 tail warning radar. Numerous operational P-51Ds had this set fitted at the end of the war and the aerials are quite clear in photographs. When modeling

such a kit remember that the array consisted of a fore and aft rod and a central loop. As such an addition can be a little delicate it is best to fix it to the inside face of each fin half before assembly. In this way whatever material is chosen, either plastic or fine wire, it can be anchored firmly.

RECYCLING

With the foregoing comments in mind it is clear that the avid modeler will inevitably accumulate a stack of kits that are at best superseded by other newer one or are in general terms unusable, at least on the face of it. I found this with the P-40. Having acquired numerous 1/72-scale kits of the type over the years I found the Monogram P-40N was there in abundance in my abandoned boxes. My liking for late-war fighters in general was the reason for this, that and the fact that no P-40N was otherwise available – in any scale – for decades. I built a few of the Monogram offerings but neglected to carry out the modifications necessary to bring the kit up to a more reasonable standard. Was there still a use for a kit that was not only overscale but also quite basic in that when the large rivets were sanded away all trace of the flying surfaces disappeared too? As the images in this chapter show, when things don't turn out as expected or hoped, all need not be lost.

ONE SEAT OR TWO?

One of the most aesthetically appealing of the wartime fighter trainer conversions, the P-40

Warhawk came as a dual seater in a number of guises. The most ambitious was the reworking of a number of P-40Ns to accommodate a second cockpit behind the existing one with a clear Perspex section linking the two, plus a few other detail additions. One such is what I can best describe as a fuselage side plate adjacent to the second cockpit plus an elevated mirror device mounted above the front hood to enable the instructor to see what the pupil was pushing and pulling during the flight.

I converted the Monogram P-40N into the TP-40N without too much trouble. An Eastern European manufacturer known as LF Models released a 1/72-scale TP-40N sometime in 1999 – but the object of the exercise was to show that you can recycle old ones.

Kits of other American fighters can be adapted to trainer configuration, the early razor-back Thunderbolt and Mustang looking the best in my view. The P-47Ds used for this purpose had elongated cockpit glazing in some instances, while the stillborn TP-47G, only two of which were built, had the standard cockpit moved forward a few feet. It was not selected for production but those P-47s used as front-line trainers had extra glazing aft of the standard cockpit. The single-seat versions that sired such aircraft can be readily adapted, the addition of a second seat being simple enough using kits in the most popular scales.

Examples of the early Mustangs were also adapted to trainer configuration in a similar way to the other types, the P-51B/C having extended aft glazing to the greenhouse canopy while in the field modifications to the P-51D to accommodate two people resulted in the canopy sometimes being cut into three sections.

BELOW After these modifications, the model was painted and the smaller details were reinstalled. These details were repainted too. A hobby stand was used to hold the model upside down while the details on the lower surface of the model were added.

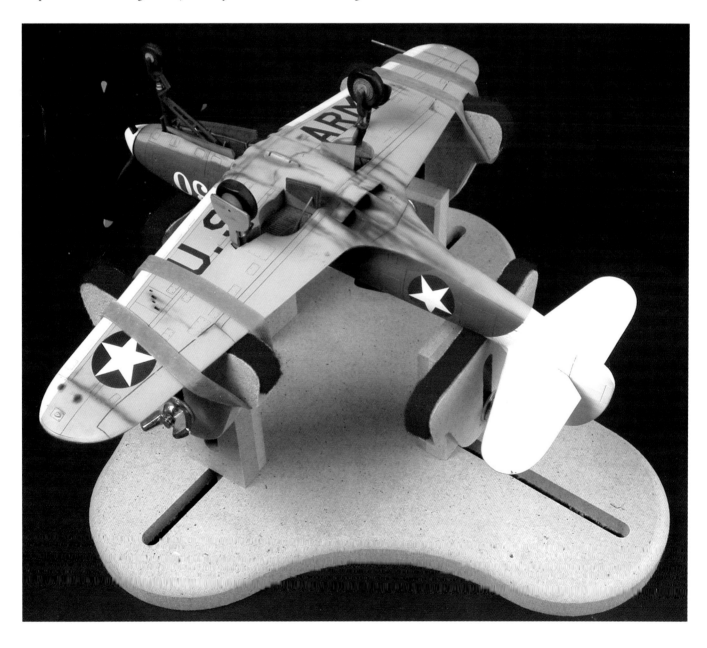

RIGHT The only other addition to the kit was a set of six-stack exhausts from Ultracast. The starboard door was glued in the open position. The attractive decals were sourced from Cutting Edge Decal set CED48146, Airacobra #4.

Of all the trainer conversions of Mustangs, the P-51B is probably the most satisfying in modeling terms with the added attraction of some unusual color schemes, such as the overall red used on one example flown by the 4th Fighter Group.

Two seats were occasionally added under the wartime P-51D's huge canopy and there was also a TP-51D, which had an elongated hood designed to give the second occupant greater headroom.

At the other end of the fighter trainer spectrum was the quite odd looking TP-39Q. With a second canopy perched on the nose forward of the original, the result was not only the worst looking two-seat conversion but in my view the world's most ugly aircraft!

Moving up to the Bell P-63, this had at least in a projected trainer version, a second cockpit added in the fuselage aft of the standard position, making it another candidate for a two-seat fighter conversion. Like almost anything associated with the wartime USAAF the model possibilities are much wider than they may seem as first sight.

CHAPTER 5
ADVANCED CONSTRUCTION

The questions of modeling skill level and task difficulty are hard to quantify with absolute precision: the answer has surely to come from a personal viewpoint. That kits carry labels stating that the contents are intended for different levels of modeling expertise surely does not inhibit the purchase – yet some people may find that the complexity of the components, particularly the multi-media type kit, indeed represents a task more difficult than imagined.

Some accessory kits have now reached the stage that used to be more associated with model engineering. They incorporate a range of non plastic parts that require a different approach to attaching such minute components as flap hinges, oleo scissors and dive brakes. These after-market kits are fine for those who require such ultra-fine detail but certain aspects of modeling seem still to be a challenge as regards the final, generally external, effect.

Some often prefer to see greater emphasis placed on the external finish, areas that can be viewed when the model is completed such as gun bay doors, stores racks and other "things under wings" than parts that may well be hidden away under cowlings and so forth. The argue that most USAAF fighters give little choice to view the interior however detailed a kit may be unless the modeler resorts to artificial cutaways or a complete strip down with the airframe pared to the bone, as indeed it might have been during a major service.

However it can be rewarding to opt to focus on one or two areas of the kit. There is plenty of scope. Relatively few of the smaller scale kits have provision for open gun bays for example but cutting these out and adding new ones from Plasticard can considerably enhance the finished item – and they're far more likely to be visible than flaps, which on some aircraft at least are hardly ever seen in the down position.

Some might also argue that multi-media accessories can be disproportionately expensive and add greatly to the task of completing what may already be a fairly complex kit. Extra time will have to be spent on the building stage, which in total hours, can almost double. However, multi-media accessories are very much up to the individual modeler, who must choose the one or two that will enhance a particularly favored, detailed project. By no

BOTTOM The AMtech 1/48-scale Curtiss P-40F Warhawk, modeled by Brett Green. During the early 1990s, AMT released a series of 1/48-scale P-40 Warhawks that were quite accurate in outline but somewhat basic in detail. They earned a reputation for challenging fit, especially around the wing roots and the engine cowl access panels. Other Warhawk/Kittyhawk variants were developed by AMT but, for unknown reasons, were never released. In 2002, a new company called AMtech finally used the first of these unreleased molds to launch their P-40E Warhawk/Kittyhawk Mk Ia. The P-40F Kittyhawk II was powered by a license-built version of the famous Rolls-Royce Merlin engine. This development was intended to improve high-altitude performance of the P-40, which was greatly inferior to its Axis contemporaries. However, in the final analysis, performance was only marginally improved. The P-40L was a further development of the Merlin equipped Warhawk. This type was intended to be lightweight (with the reduction of equipment, including the deletion of two wing-mounted machine guns) and therefore faster. The disappointing result was an increase in speed of only around four miles per hour. Many P-40Ls were later retrofitted with the extra two wing guns. Very early P-40Fs and Ls had the same short fuselage as the P-40E. Later production machines featured a longer fuselage and repositioned horizontal tailplanes. AMtech launched their P-40F/L "long tail" version in early 2003. This new company was not happy with the profile and detail of the fuselage nose as molded by AMT. AMtech therefore commissioned a new, accurate solid resin nose to be included in their kit. This permitted modelers who were not happy with the shape of the kit nose to cut it off and replace it. Less experienced modelers could simply build the kit with the plastic fuselage intact. In the modeling project that appears in this chapter, we will use the resin nose, address some of the fit challenges and add a detailed replacement cockpit to the model.

means should the less experienced be persuaded to buy all and sundry extras: should they prove difficult or frustrating to incorporate into a kit, the modeling community might lose another would-be convert.

However, on the other hand, as the images that accompany this chapter show, the extra time and effort dedicated to adding advanced modeling detail to a kit, and the experience and confidence gained as a result, can make such projects very worthwhile indeed.

CHALLENGING THE MODELER

In the following pages of this chapter, we'll attempt to highlight those areas of each of the classic US fighter models of World War 2 that always seem to need special attention, and more advanced modeling skills as a result, irrespective of the kit and to some extent the scale.

Beginning at the front, the propeller(s) of all wartime fighters bear scrutiny, as these vary to a surprising degree even between the same aircraft type to the same scale. Different manufacturers naturally design their propeller components in a variety of ways although some time ago there was simply one, an integral spinner with the blades attached. These days, propeller blades are increasingly presented as three or four separate items plus at least two more for the front of the spinner and its back plate. The latter is usually molded with pick-up points to hold the blades rigidly in position – but this can provide a challenge insofar as you need to manually set the angle of each one. There is some flexibility here of course but do check several photos to get typical blade angles correct.

Two-piece spinners are relatively straightforward on aircraft such as the P-40, P-38 and P-51, with the proviso to ensure that both halves go together without an annoying step that may be difficult to sand smooth once the blades are in position.

Should you feel that the propeller blades supplied in a certain kit are undersized there are several after-market alternatives. The US Kendall Model Company (KMC) of Miami offers one. I have two of their resin Curtiss propeller blade sets for 1/48-scale P-47s that are excellent. The pointed-blade type is adaptable to very many Thunderbolt kits that may have the blades a little too short.

I spray propeller blades almost any color other than straight black. By adding a minute amount of blue, green or brown to matt black (the latter not stirred up completely so as to retain a sheen), propellers will look suitably different to other black areas of the kit. Don't forget the reverse faces, particularly where photographic evidence shows the blade paint to have been worn away by the effects of slipstream-blasted sand. Aircraft based in desert areas often lost paint from propeller blades and several references show the effect to advantage.

I have a small horror of kit instructions that simply tell you paint several areas – blades, tires, guns and some cockpit interior instruments – black. I often wonder how many people end up with models that look most odd in this respect.

PLASTIC HORSEPOWER

Detailing engines is a subject in itself and many modelers of US fighters end up with a sizeable stock of Pratt & Whitney, Rolls-Royce or Allison engines, which are not always incorporated in the kit if it can be completed without the extra work power-plant detailing entails. Most manufacturers producing kits in scales from 1/48 upwards provide at least a rudimentary engine block if only as an anchorage point for the exhausts. If the engine is used, few self-respecting modelers would dream of letting it be viewed without some additions.

Wartime piston engines were complex and exhibited masses of pipes, supports, fuel lines and wiring, some of which are visible even with a single panel removed, so again it is up to individual taste as to how much extra work is put in on a part of a kit that can otherwise be hidden – or treated as a separate component in its own right. Suffice to say that if extra engine detail is undertaken, the result can often be most impressive.

For the sake of economy, some smaller kit engines have what would be separate items such as electrical leads or small diameter pipes, molded into the plastic block, so these should be carefully removed and replaced with new brass etch, thin wire or stretched sprue components to give a more realistic three-dimensional effect.

Engine bearers or mountings on wartime US Army fighters consisted of quite substantial lengths of round or flat section steel, the latter often being drilled out to save weight. All the larger scale kits incorporate these distinctive pieces, as do several in 1/48 scale.

If the kit is designed in such a way that leaving out the engine involves adding blanking plates behind the exhaust ports and maybe some internal bracing, the engine might just as

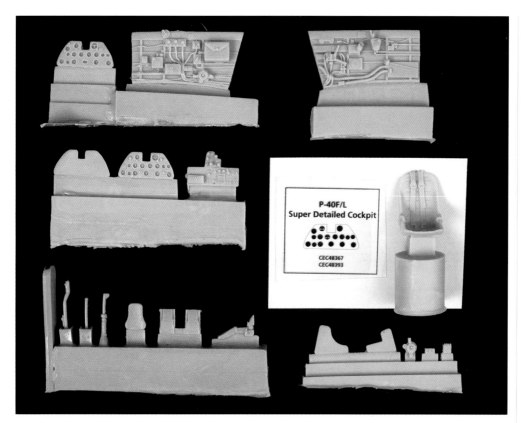

well be used and enhanced a little. Going a step further and deciding to show the work via detached inspection panels will, as many modelers will know, involve reducing the thickness of the plastic. As they come, most plastic parts have over-scale edges to allow the adhesive to be applied. This entirely practical approach does not however allow realistic display of removed panels without some work with scalpel and file.

A study of many of the fine references to aircraft power plants, particularly the Walk Around and Detail in Scale series of books, will reveal (apart from many small ancillary items that can be incorporated in the engine area) thin metal strips around all the main inspection panels. These were punched at intervals to accept rivets and hold the removable panels in place. Such strips are hard to fit after much assembly has taken place, so for an engine detailing project they should be added first.

This is not necessarily because all the panels are to be refitted but the fact that the support strips show up as bright yellow chromate on many reference photos. Miss them out and the lack will surely be obvious, as will the fact that they are set too far in if the plastic walls have not been thinned down.

In addition to preparing the bays to make them more realistic, work on the engine itself can be as extensive as the individual modeler wishes.

Clearly there are many who detail engines in 1/72 scale as if the work was second nature but personally I prefer to reserve this activity for the larger scale kit. Eyesight may well play a part here, but to some of us the larger kit can be that much more impressive because you can more readily observe the work carried out. It is of course perfectly possible to pick at engine detailing, i.e. to do just that amount of work to show what goes on under one panel on one side of the fuselage, as indeed many kits recommend.

Many kits inspire you to go several stages further than the raw materials supplied. I find this to be particularly true in 1/32-scale kits, some of which represent only the raw material for an endless amount of super detailing in various area of the airframe. Depending on the configuration of the full-size aircraft, there will be various sections of intake trunking, associated mesh dust filters, as well wiring, that can be incorporated by scratch building.

The P-40 is a case in point. It is fascinating to see how for example, the engine cooling system worked on this fighter when the entire front end is exposed. The modeler could be inspired to build up the three circular air intakes under the engine proper and add as much additional detail as possible.

Either of the two 1/24 scale Mustang kits, which contain an impressive number of pieces to build up the main block, supercharger,

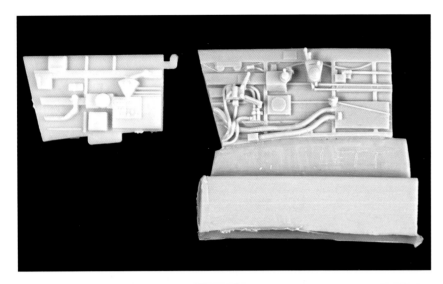

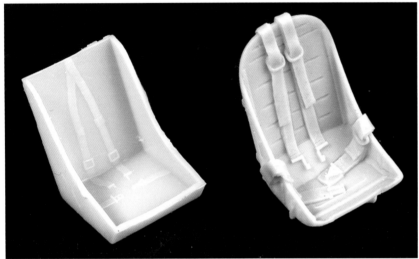

ABOVE TOP It is possible for experienced modelers to scratch build details for their models, but the current generation of resin accessories offers a supreme level of detail combined with simplicity and speed of assembly. Compare the difference in detail and fidelity between the kit sidewall (left) and the resin replacement sidewall (right).

ABOVE The pilot's seat is usually the most obvious feature inside the aircraft. Apart from the more accurate shape, the resin seat in this cockpit set (right) includes a clever representation of the pressed metal ribs (on the front and back of the seat), and an authentically draped harness. The kit's seat is also shown here, on the left.

ancillaries and mountings for a convincing Packard Merlin are good for this.

Mention of engines and exposed panels bring us to what the model will look like with much of its interior on show. American fighters, unlike their German counterparts, generally did not have a plethora of hinges from which to hang the panels. No doubt we've all admired models of Bf 109s or FW 190s with every access panel open while still being, so to speak, in one piece. The Germans employed the universally excellent Zeus fasteners so that inspection panels, often quite large ones, merely hung down (or were braced upwards) with the aid of stays. They usually remained attached to the aircraft – not so with the Allies. The P-38s should gain an honorable mention as an exception in this respect as its nose panels hinged upwards to allow access to the gun bay.

This means, in modeling terms, that in-line engine fighters such as the P-40 and P-51 will, if their innards are displayed, be cast instantly into diorama mode. Therefore to keep the kit display area within reasonable dimensions, the

dislocated engine panels will need to be rested against the wing or tailplane or laid out on the wing. Obviously, hinge any panels that were not normally detached and add any retaining rods necessary to hold them open if the kit sprues do not include them. If a more elaborate scene, perhaps incorporating figures, is required, then the panels may be placed on trestles or other work benches. Alternatively, they can simply be laid on the ground adjacent to the aircraft.

BATTLE DAMAGE

As part of their kit package, Monogram incorporated wing dihedral pieces in some 1/32-scale kits, an addition that could well be incorporated into a detailed model to show the wing structure in some way. Such items are useful when recreating battle damage, with some of the surface skin peeled back as it was occasionally wont to do under fire. Damaged airframes provide numerous ways for a display model to be that bit different.

Revealing what went under the skin as a result of the aircraft being struck by shot and shell does however demand that the modeler indulge in replicating portions of the basic structure to scale dimensions. This is a fascinating aspect of aircraft modeling and one that should be far removed from the Hollywood idea of a line of bullet holes stitching the skin as neatly as a sewing machine. This and other approaches to revealing what is hidden under a solid plastic exterior might be thought of as turning the clock back to the days when modeling meant building the airplane's structure first. Not so. Today the modern plastic kit is adaptable enough to provide the ideal compromise for revealing part of the structure, but the work involved can be time-consuming.

One way not to create battle damage is to make the mistake of trying to pare down plastic to a thin enough section – it'll take hours. Instead cut away the entire panel(s) and substitute thin sections of Plasticard suitably torn and holed. More card may be cut and shaped into part of the airframe longerons under the skin. When trapping this new structural effect between two wing sections, you can cheat a little by supporting it on the existing lower section, which remains as it comes in the kit.

The vertical fins of fighters often took flak or cannon shell hits that peeled back the skin, and this effect may be created without difficulty. Either study the photos of a particular aircraft in order to reproduce exactly a damage pattern with specific markings or complete the model with typical damage. For a diorama of wing damage, how about placing a pilot figure with his head and shoulder poking through the hole?

Many model dioramas go for a crash landing – one fighter displayed on a baseboard invariably with its prop blades bent back, and maybe, without wings and other items. A pilot or ground crew figure may be in attendance at the wreck. But such *tableaux* do not always completely convince. The modeler should get a feel for not only where crash-landed aircraft break, but also how they break – simply hacking the pieces off will not look convincing.

Bending back the prop blades is probably the simplest form of battle damage, but even this needs to be done correctly. One method is to heat the blades gently over a naked flame, just sufficient to make them pliable enough to bend. You may want at the same time to twist them off center. Keep the reference to hand as you carry out the creative vandalism and you should be pleased with the result. It goes without saying that you should test the method first, and then perhaps use an old prop with poorly-shaped blades for the display model rather than sacrifice a good one.

If none of the foregoing attracts you, there is another way: the Japanese company Bandai suggested that after completing their 1/24 scale P-51D the modeler wishing to show off some of the interior could take a hot knife to it. The instruction sheet duly showed a kit with its canopy cut into and the aircraft's center section partially exposed after a jagged edge chunk had been removed.

The view will often be taken that detailing an engine and perhaps adding items such as ground transport, servicing stands and figures, puts the model firmly into the diorama category. This will often be the view of show organizers and judges, should the model be required for entry in a competition. Extra work will of course be required to broaden out what may have started out as a single, relatively simple aircraft project, so plan in advance what you want to achieve with any kit you tackle. Numerous scenes will suggest themselves from the pages of suitable books and magazines dealing with wartime fighter operations.

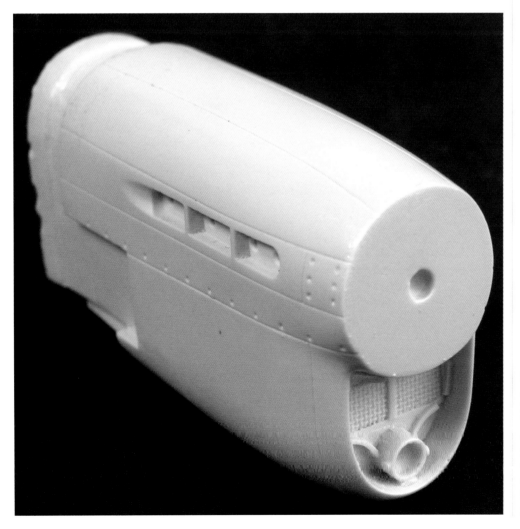

LEFT The solid resin nose on AMtech's P-40F/L is cast in a hard, cream-colored material. The distinctive intake inside the chin of the cowl is beautifully rendered as a deep undercut in this single part. Panel lines are crisply recessed, matching the high-quality surface texture on the kit's plastic parts.

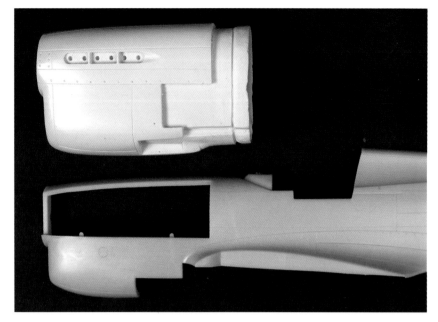

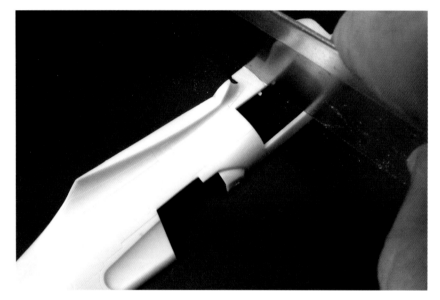

ABOVE TOP Some of the differences in shape and panel location can be seen in this comparison between the resin nose and its plastic counterpart. The resin casting plug, as indicated by the vertical line at the back of the part, must be sawn off to achieve the proper fit inside the kit fuselage.

ABOVE The kit fuselage halves are marked and a razor saw is used to make the two short cuts per side required for the conversion. When you are marking and cutting, always cut a little less off than you think will be required. It is easier to trim before fitting than filling and sanding a gap afterwards!

If a number of items are to be detached from the model for display purposes, the builder may well opt for a diorama type exhibit by placing the aircraft on a suitable base. A diorama does not of course have to extend to the ultimate realism of greasy mechanics, oil drums, bowsers, engine hoists and work stands but merely a neat group of detached parts displayed, preferably to show off any markings. On the other hand, replicating a full size servicing scene is an attractive proposition, so again the final design of the display is to the modeler's choosing.

FAMOUS FIGHTERS

If we look at the salient design points of the various USAAF fighters, we find obvious areas that should when duplicated on a model be 100 per cent accurate if the final result is to be convincing. These areas come into what might be termed the "make or break" category. Taking the models through in numerical order of designation it is easy to identify where each could fall down if these basics are overlooked. Although the world's manufacturers currently seem bent on reproducing all the main combat fighters in all their sub-types, plus prototypes, one-offs and even "paper planes" in kit form, we can't cover them all here. Of those aircraft projects that were allocated type numbers, relatively few actually entered full-scale production for USAAC/USAAF service. As noted in Table 1 on page 44, the rest existed only as prototypes or pre-service test examples.

SEVERSKY P-35

Although its was a late-1930s, pre-war design, the P-35 was one of several obsolescent fighters that found what modest fame it garnered under US colors during the debacle in the Philippines. Overtaken technically as well as tactically by the rampaging Japanese, the P-35 tried valiantly to hold off the likes of the Mitsubishi A6M which swept over Clark Field in the early hours of 8 December. Overwhelmed by the opposition, US pilots nevertheless gave it back in enough measure for the modern modeler to include the type in a representative fighter collection.

Color schemes for both NMF and camouflaged examples may be found for the little Seversky, well exemplifying the US transition from peace to war after Pearl Harbor. As with the P-36, Hobbycraft and Academy seem to have followed each other to release the P-35 in 1/48 scale, there being little to choose between them in terms of fine surface detail. I feel that the Academy has captured well the contours of the P-35, and reproduced the hump-backed appearance of the original with its modest dimensions. Molded in light gray plastic Academy's kit is very delicate – to the point of being adversely affected by any rubbing down of joint lines. Surface scratches that would normally disappear on other kits persist on the P-35, so a heavy-handed approach will cause problems, particularly if an NMF scheme is chosen.

CURTISS P-36

A rugged and mean performer, the P-36 found arguably more fame in French and Finnish rather than American hands. But as one of the few USAAC fighters that managed to knock down some of the Japanese attackers on December 7, 1941 it has an indisputable place in aviation's mythical hall of fame. A fine exhibit in the USAF Museum at Dayton, Ohio now represents the actual aircraft of the 18th PG that claimed the first aerial victories. Having thus been widely seen this particular P-36 might be too familiar for many modelers – but there are alternatives. Even if your model theme is to be strictly post Day of Infamy, enough color schemes can be found.

Several P-36 kits have appeared over the years with Monogram leading the field with a neat 1/72-scale rendering many moons ago. Hobbycraft and Academy have released a total of four 1/48-scale Hawks, all of which are satisfying to build. The aircraft lends itself to numerous well-documented USAAC markings schemes, a selection of which are available on commercial decal sheets, among them AeroMaster.

Tackling the Academy P-36A represents few problems, provided that the instructions concerning the mounting of the engine are followed to the letter. Failure to do this can result in the cowling not fitting over the engine, which is actually designed to be positioned too far back. The mounting boss needs to be lengthened to ensure this error is remedied. These minor drawbacks apart, this kit, which lacks some cockpit detail, will be snapped up by those who wish to add it. Alternatively it is attractive enough to be built straight out of the box.

In 1/72 the P-36 has fared quite well, also being produced in this scale by Frog and Hasegawa, among others. Not having examined any of the smaller scale kits I can't really pass on any comments as to their accuracy. I'm sure then that Bert Kinsey, author of the excellent "Detail in Scale" series of books, won't mind if I borrow a few observations from his review section in the first volume of a two-parter covering the P-40 variants. Regarding the smaller scales it would appear that Bert and his review team plump for the Monogram kit as the yardstick against which all others are measured.

P-38 LIGHTNING

In common with most US fighter kits, contemporary models of the P-38 are quite comprehensive, the aircraft generally being scaled down well. Assuming that the more experienced modeler has decided to work with one of the latest 1/48-scale offerings from Hasegawa or Academy, there won't be much to complain about.

As with any kit, detail can be added to the cockpit area: the Lightning's canopy featured roll down windows on each side and a roof

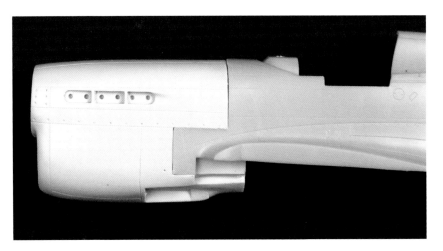

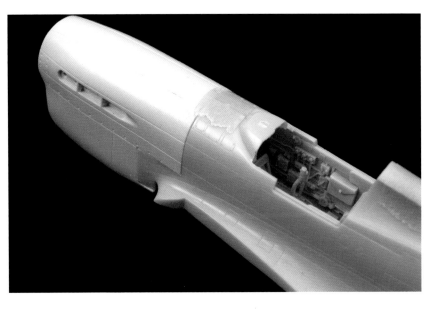

section, which was hinged to flip up and back. Faced with a one-piece model canopy the traditional method of enhancing a P-38 as a display model was to tackle the delicate job of separating each section and displaying them all in the open position. Today the modeler can often lay aside the razor saw as the canopy parts are often already separated. In addition, the better kits will enable the nose gun magazines to be fully or partially exposed under separate doors, and some engine detail will be visible via separate panels. The list of accessories from Verlinden, Kendall Model Co or Missing Link Models, to name but a few, can usually supply super-detail extras for more than one variant of the P-38. The scale of the original aircraft has a bearing on what is available for model kits and as a rule of thumb 1/48 scale offers slightly greater scope.

More aware than ever before of the conversion possibilities with one basic airframe, the mainstream manufacturers often revise their kits to offer more variants, particularly if they are similar in most other respects. The shape of

ABOVE TOP **Constant test fitting is an essential procedure to achieving a perfect fit. In this picture, we can see that there are only a few minimal gaps before trimming and sanding.**

ABOVE **This view provides a more complete picture. Note the slight step between the top-rear of the resin nose and the fuselage, and the ridge at the bottom of the nose. There are two ways to deal with these minor problems. We can glue the parts as they are and sand the parts until they match; or we can adjust the parts to fit when they are glued. Excessive filling and sanding can lead to loss of surface details so we will be making a few more adjustments before assembly. The cockpit parts have also been test-fitted to ensure that they do not interfere with the resin nose.**

the engine cowlings instantly distinguishes a P-38F/H from a P-38J/L but there are more subtle differences that the kit tool makers may not necessarily have picked up.

Given all these integral component parts, the advanced conversion possibilities are relatively few with the P-38 as the two distinctly different types of cowling for the Allison engines have been kitted a number of times, as has the radar-equipped, night fighter twin seater, the P-38M. As the "last of the Lightnings" just missed aerial combat, the interest factor for some modelers will understandably be borderline – but the aircraft does look impressive and makes an interesting comparison with the P-61 – in an equally battered finish. Available photos show that the finish of the P-38M suffered almost as much weathering as its earlier counterpart after a few weeks in the Pacific. The books tell us that the two-seat M left the US in a glossier shade of black but it seemed not to have lasted too well.

The radar-equipped P-38M's all-black color scheme lends itself to further comparison with an early model P-38F/H similarly finished in a matt night fighter scheme. Placed alongside the camouflaged day fighters, this would be a nice contrast. The early Lightning variants saw some limited Pacific combat as a stop gap pending the delivery of sufficient P-61s.

Monogram were once again the first manufacturer to see the attraction of a "night Lightning" and offered it as an alternative version to their P-38L as long ago as 1966. Beautifully riveted and paneled, the detail is all raised, but this can to turned to advantage. The kit includes some crystal clear transparencies to go over the raised second seat of the P-38M. I recently found details of one of four aircraft that reached Japan after the end of the war and saw service with the 418th and 421st Night Fighter Squadrons, a good modeling topic.

As one might expect, the climate wrought havoc on the paintwork of these machines. You might reproduce this finish with a coat of black over the silver plastic, lightly sanded to bring out those raised rivets and panels.

In common with other aircraft with a nosewheel configuration, the Lightning looks to my mind very impressive with the nosewheel turned a few degrees off center. This is a personal thing, but one that many modelers will surely understand. Not that model firms readily indulge me in this: they hardly ever separate the oleo legs or mold the forks at an angle to make the display of a turned nosewheel easy. This is invariably on the grounds that the model's nosewheel fork section would be even weaker than it already is. Any weight put on the

leg to balance the model would probably be singularly unsuccessful.

As with any tricycle undercarriage aircraft, the problem of weighting the nose of a P-38 can be acute, as no modeler worth his salt would dream of resorting to a transparent tail prop to keep all three wheels on the ground. Adding nose weight to a model with an angled nosewheel might be a disaster, so the best solution may be to circumvent this and attach the model to a baseboard.

All in all, P-38s such as that from Academy, Hasegawa and Hobbycraft in 1/48 may safely be assembled and finished quite quickly, although the second of the manufacturers listed have apparently built in quite a construction challenge to their P-38J. Judging from some reviews, aligning the tail booms is particularly tricky which might result in a switch to the Academy kits, which are simpler in this respect. The choice though is not easy as the detail of the Hasegawa Lightning is said to be excellent.

One curious item I found on the Academy kit is two mysterious bulges on the inside faces of the engine cowlings. I've checked thoroughly without finding similar protuberances on the full-size aircraft and can only assume that the toolmakers misinterpreted the brightly polished oval seen on the skin of almost all Lightnings at that point. These highly polished ovals acted as mirrors for the pilot to check that the nosewheel was "down and locked" and were of course flat.

Another area that needs attending to on the P-38 is the guns. Most model manufacturers repeatedly mold these with the slotted barrel jackets visible, irrespective of the version. In fact the guns of later production Lightnings were set into blast tubes, as per the P-47. That said, it is a pity to change these as blast tubes are quite plain and can tend to indicate that the modeler has not bothered to fit more detailed guns to his kit. Faced with such a "can't win" situation, individual modelers might opt for a little artistic license and fit the kit guns, which usually have exposed barrel jackets.

Literally the biggest challenge to detailing a P-38 lies with the 1/32-scale kit from Revell. It definitely needs to have all the raised rivet detail removed and the main panel lines and the flying surfaces re-scribed. After a few applications of wet and dry, the rather thin plastic trailing edges (no complaint there!) of the wings and tailplane lose a little of their crispness and some detail may need to be redefined around the trim tabs

On this kit the entire nose pod – unusually for a P-38 kit – is a separate assembly, making any additional features or the application of nose art, names and scoreboards, that much simpler. No internal parts are supplied for the ammunition magazines or the gun breeches and in this size there is an almost irresistible urge to super-detail this area. After that there's only the cockpit interior to tackle, the kit providing a basic floor and sidewall components to start you off. The advantage of being able to work on the nose before the huge wings are attached becomes obvious with the kit to hand.

P-39 AIRACOBRA

In a field full of tail draggers, the Airacobra stands alone among first-line US single-engine fighters by having a tricycle landing gear. This again creates the potential problem of persuading it to stand correctly on its nosewheel. Weighting the extreme forward fuselage can result in similar problems you may experience with the P-38 so again, the solution could be locating the finished model on a baseboard and lightly anchoring each wheel with a pin, adhesive or sticky tape. Three-pointing the tricycle landing gear of the Airacobra applies equally to the other two "twins" – the P-61 and P-70, should your representative collection of USAAF types extend to multi-engine aircraft and night fighters.

In 1969 a 1/48-scale P-39 was released by Monogram to take and hold the "best kit" slot for this particular type for many years. Providing build options for a P-400 and three P-39s (a D-1, D-2 and L-1, the last in Russian markings) the Airacobra remains an excellent subject to work with today. Having only recently been joined by two other P-39s in this scale, a resin conversion kit from Missing Link Models and an injection molded example from Eduard (see Chapter 4), the radical Bell fighter has not exactly swamped the display tables in competition. This may also be that the P-39 is perceived as the least effective US single-seater, plus the fact that its markings have been rather poorly documented, with a few notable exceptions.

The Monogram kit provides useful internal detail in the nose area, the forward bay of which was dominated by the barrel and breech of a 37mm or 20mm cannon. The kit interior makes an extra case for mounting the P-39 on a baseboard rather than adding ballast, as to make room for the amount needed to keep the nosewheel on the ground, some of the gun detail would have to be dropped. This is a pity because the internals of the P-39 may be finished to look quite convincing even with no further detail added.

A bulky weight stuffed into the nose of any model risks sacrificing some internal parts and might reduce the opportunity to show the panels opened up, more so with the P-39 due to its configuration. There is very little space forward and although it is possible to place a weight forward of the nosewheel without sacrificing the interior, you'll be hard put to find material with enough density to balance the model.

A drawback with all early Monogram kits, the P-39 being no exception, is the raised panel lines. All these should be sanded off, not only on the grounds of authenticity but the practical one of getting decals to lay down over raised inspection panels, lines and rivets. Again the "light sand" can be employed so that some raised detail can show through the paint.

SMALLER AIRACOBRA

Revell represented the P-39 fairly well in 1/72 scale many years in advance of its rivals. Old now and with its parts covered in rivets, the kit suffered from a too shallow outline shape, but was deemed a little better than the more angular profile of the Airfix and Heller kits released some time later. The latter kits do however have a number of parts that may be used to enhance one of the three offerings if a representative Airacobra is required in this scale. Areas to take note of include the undercarriage, armament and any engine access panels.

As with many vintage kits the cockpit transparency in any of these P-39s may look decidedly forlorn. It is a fact that some transparencies in this scale were not very clear even when they were first kitted and subsequent pressings have done nothing to improve the molds. This factor, along with overly heavy framing, makes them prime candidates for replacement. But using three kits and a decent canopy an acceptable P-39 can result.

Many of us who have these older kits on our shelves sometimes find that a newer release is not necessarily that much of an improvement to justify a purchase, leading us to drag out that dusty box again, along with all the spares. This is certainly true for the P-39. As there have been relatively few of them in any scale, the "old but good" adage may well hold true.

BELL P-63

The Kingcobra was a fascinating development of the P-39 and offers an attractive comparison to its older stable mate. Although sharing a similar configuration, the two aircraft were quite different in detail – revised nosewheel oleo, four-bladed propeller, new tail surfaces and dorsal rear fuselage in the case of the P-63C and pylon-mounted guns rather than integral wing mountings on all versions.

For years the only representation of the "King" in plastic kit form was a 1/72-scale kit by the Japanese firm Aoshima. Shortly before this book went to press however MPM and Toko added the P-63 to their 1/72-scale injection-molded ranges. The vacuformed kits from Wings of the US are reportedly very good, though this type of kit demands more from the modeler in all stages of construction than is necessary with injection molded parts.

MPM has also extended its short-run range to a P-63 in 1/48 scale. Fit of parts leaves something to be desired and as is usual with limited run kits there is much cleaning up to be

undertaken before construction commences. Afterwards you can look forward to wielding the filler to close the gaps.

CURTISS P-40

This type is dealt with specifically in the images that accompany this chapter, but it is worth detailing some more gereneric points too on the aircraft, and the modeling products available.

Adding detail to a P-40 model will usually begin with the air intake and the cooling flaps at the lower rear end of the engine bay. These have been molded fully closed, fully open and

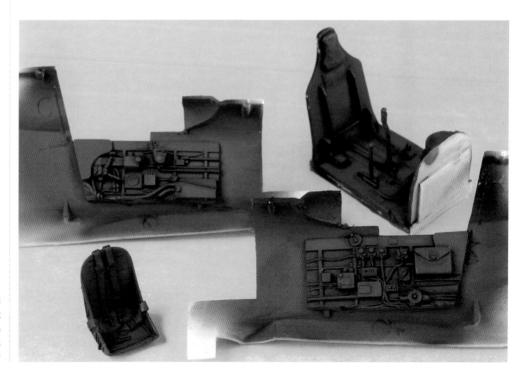

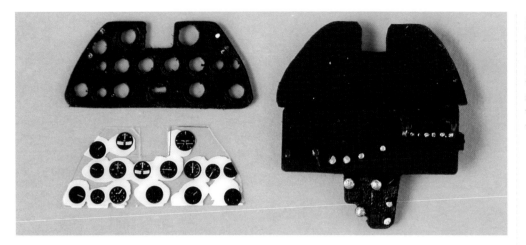

partially open, separately or integral, depending on the kit in question. Moving back from this area, the belly rack for a bomb or drop tanks may have to be added or at least improved by essential detail. Fortunately perhaps from a modeling viewpoint, USAAF Warhawks tended to have a neater set of four sway braces to hold bombs in place than did Kittyhawks of the RAF, with their extraordinary cat's cradle of angle iron hanging between the oleos.

The wheels of the real P-40 were almost disproportionately large and in common with other aircraft, they were usually fitted with treaded tires. You would not have thought this to be the case as far as kit manufacturers were concerned as for years they persisted in supplying only smooth tires in their P-40 kits. If the subject you are working on had those lovely diamond-patterned tires (and the kit ones don't)

an effort should be made to cut the tread in. A better alternative these days is to search the custom parts lists of the specialist suppliers who may well offer a set of tires with the correct treads in resin or other material. This is marginally easier in the smaller scales as 1/32 scale accessories remain in somewhat limited supply. Don't cut kit tires unless you have to, but on the other hand, don't complete a P-40 with completely "bald" tires, as it just won't look right.

Of all the Warhawk kits produced it is rather strange that the majority of them have been of the P-40E. Notwithstanding the manufacturers' obsession with the marketing opportunities of the sharkmouthed Flying Tigers, this appears a strange imbalance, as the original AVG flew, of course, the P-40B. It appeared at one time that no kit supplier worth

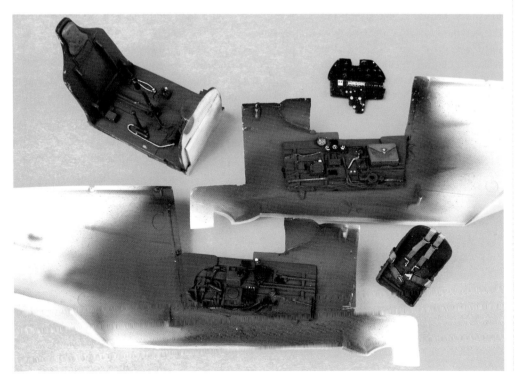

RIGHT Careful painting of
straps and buckles can result in
a very convincing seat.
A well-painted pilot's seat looks
great through an open canopy.

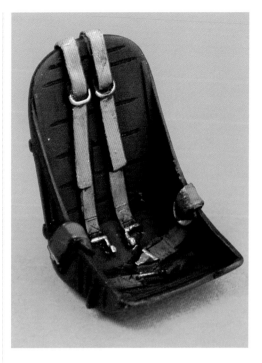

his salt could bear to release a Warhawk that did not feature a sharkmouthed aircraft on the box top, forgetting that most of the buyers had been there before.

There are now several P-40B and P-40N kits but the version that runs a close second to the E model in US service, the F, was for years all but ignored as an injection molded kit subject. This version, shown in the photographs in the this chapter, powered by a Rolls-Royce Merlin, lacked the characteristic intake on top of the nose and had different engine cowling contours to the Allison-engine machines. Other variations of the Warhawk, the K and L, were similarly ignored as kits until recently, that gap being plugged by releases in both 1/48 and 1/72 scales.

AeroMaster's conversion kit for the P-40F comes as a small box containing a new nose, flaps and rudder and fin fillet sections. Designed for mating with the truncated fuselage of the Mauve P-40N the conversion works a treat and opens up a far wider range of markings possibilities than hitherto. The one drawback for the lazy modeler used more to completing American fighters in OD and Neutral Gray is that the vast majority of P-40Fs in service (mainly in the MTO) wore two-tone RAF-retile camouflage.

The P-40F and L were built as "short" and "long" fuselage versions and were widely used by American air forces, a fact that makes their omission from kit lists for so long an even greater mystery, but better late than never. Using the AeroMaster conversion set and other kits such as AMTech's recent release, the modeler now has the opportunity to build virtually the entire front-line P-40 range.

REVELL'S P-40 IN 1/32

As it comes the original Revell kit lends itself to numerous P-40Es in service with the 5th Air Force as well as the latter day Flying Tigers during their transitional period to become part of the 23d Fighter Group of the 14th Air Force. This particular unit also used the short fuselage P-40K, so adding a fin fillet to the kit expands the markings horizon a bit further. Decals for Warhawks in this scale are not very numerous so a resort to masking and spraying will be the only option for some camouflage schemes. In any event decals in this size can be rather obvious, so a "direct on" painting approach should bring about a more satisfying result.

As it comes out of the box, the Revell P-40E box is one of the best of the single-seaters featured in the original 1/32 scale fighter series. One reason is that unsightly pins either to attach the transparent parts to the fuselage or to hold opening sections in place do not mar the canopy. I wanted to hand paint some personal artwork and employ stencils rather than decals for the national insignia, so this was an ideal kit to start with.

The surface detailing is restrained enough to bear only lightly rubbing down after a coat of paint, Revell having captured the unique "planking" effect of the Warhawk's fuselage construction well. The engine and some of the cockpit detail is convincing enough and although some vicious flash was present on some of the sprues, my overall impression was of a kit worth taking time over.

As work proceeds, you find yourself adding detail rather than having to resort to the sort of remedial work that can be a real chore. Mind you, such is necessary. "Adding" includes the stays which held the P-40's ventral engine gills open (they are molded in this position on the kit), refining the drop tank supports and adding the flexible fuel lines, generally improving the tank by sandwiching the two halves provided with a thin Plasticard seam down the middle, and in my case, cutting out one of the wing bays that held the machine gun ammunition. This necessitated adding the split doors and their retaining rods, plus some of the ammo. *In situ* in their bays the familiar belts of 0.50in. cartridges were partially hidden by covers similar to those that were supplied with Hasegawa's F6F Hellcat kit and I inserted some of these on the Warhawk after making up the walls of the bay as an elongated Plasticard box.

If you do undertake this "one wing only" cutout, don't forget to choose the right wing as you don't necessarily want to cut a decal or complicate stenciling of the national insignia. My own choice was dictated more for speed than anything else, and I opened up the gun bay on one wing only. Talking of guns, those on the P-40E and later versions were actually inserted into the wing from below via that huge panel that hinges down at the front. Anyone who has assembled a P-40 will have noticed these panels (one per wing) because they had a couple of curious shaped "swellings" at the rear, as though someone had miscalculated the true depth of the gun breeches and had to beat out the panel until they fitted! These fairings are on almost all P-40Es – except (of course) the large scale Revell one. The panels themselves are marked out but they are slightly too angled. If they are to cut out they'll both need reshaping and made squarer. Those bulged fairings: probably all the modeler can do to rectify this annoying shortcoming – short of remolding them completely – is to build them up with filler or adapt a couple of small bomb halves or other suitable item from the spares box and fair them in, taking due care to keep one eye on the references while so doing. They aren't unfortunately, very regular shapes so a particularly close eye will have to be kept on the reference photos, which are plentiful enough.

The Revell Warhawk's cockpit detail is a fertile ground for improvement, the instrument panel being a little random when it comes to the number of instruments engraved onto it. The panel includes substantial supporting "legs" on each side which do not seem to appear on the full-size aircraft and it therefore needs some reshaping and refinement in the form of drilling out each dial and adding a clear Plasticard backing. The pilot's seat in the P-40E had a rounded top as opposed to the almost square section of the kit seat. As this is too tall as it comes, it is a simple matter to reduce and reshape it prior to attaching it onto the H-shaped support provided. The P-40 seat also had prominent horizontal ribbing whereas the Revell's are vertical.

The full size P-40E did not have a cockpit floor as such, the pilot's seat being bolted to the wing upper surface spar where it passed through the fuselage. Revell do provide a floor and I have no argument with that as it makes the cockpit sub-assembly stronger and that much easier to finish prior to attaching the fuselage halves.

The US company Scratchbuilders released a kit of resin parts to convert the Revell 1/32

P-40E into an early P-40B or C. Taking this idea a few steps further is another American based company, Craftworks of Washington, which has pressed a complete and well-researched multi-media resin based kit of the P-40C. Sufficient parts are provided to build the entire Tomahawk airframe out of resin, the kit including white metal components, a brass etched fret for some of the cockpit and landing gear detail and very welcome dry decals.

SMALLER SCALE, SAME ISSUES

The outline accuracy of Curtiss Warhawks in 1/72 scale has been variable at best. Almost everyone has had a stab at the type, mainly in terms of the Allison-engine P-40E – Airfix, Frog, Hasegawa, Heller, Matchbox, Monogram and Revell to name a few. All these manufacturers have released examples over the decades, but the kits vary and some generally fall short on several counts. Frog alone gambled that a P-40B model might be popular in this scale. It was a fine little kit if a bit basic, being released at a time when this British company won many friends with a range of delicately crafted World War 2 fighters not duplicated elsewhere for years.

That the Frog P-40B remained the only kit of this version available in any scale for decades is strange considering the international fame of the American Volunteer Group, which flew this early model for most of its existence. The model manufacturers got around that by labeling all their P-40Es as "Flying Tigers" with inevitable sharkmouth decoration, which is certainly not inappropriate for a later AVG aircraft and many others operated by the CBI/Pacific-based groups.

Offering a light and restrained raised line surface, the kit is quite straightforward to assemble with an eye needing to be kept on the fit of parts. Wing root gaps are difficult to disguise without the use of filler as the model could soon take on an over-generous degree of dihedral. That said, the kit has the potential for being turned into a first-class replica although are not the strong point and the P-40B suffers from over-thick framing.

The kit's decal options offers no surprises insofar as the suggested color schemes are for AVG and RAF aircraft. This kit does however lend itself to a wide variety of early USAAC/USAAF color schemes as most of the "traditional" fighter groups, those that would form the nucleus of a modernized air force to fight in World War 2, flew the type. In fact the P-40 is an ideal subject if one wishes to show in model form the progression of US fighter markings from the unpainted aircraft of the

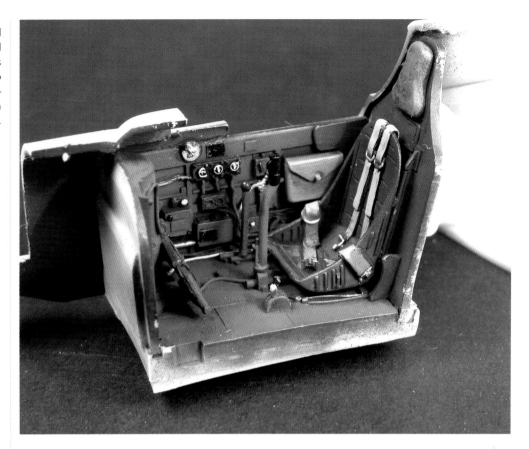

early-1940s to a similar bare metal scheme as sported by some P-40Ns in the Pacific in 1944.

Hasegawa, a company that generally produces excellent kits, next came up with a P-40N. This contained the requisite number of delicate, well detailed components to the company's typical high quality, so far removed from previous Allison-engine P-40s, most of which varied in fuselage length, canopy size, wheel dimensions and so forth.

However this particular kit, like some others in the 1/72 scale Hasegawa range, seems to be a shade undersized, particularly in fuselage depth, leading to the conclusion that the draughtsmen had miscalculated the dimensions on this occasion. Of course it could be that manufacturers other than Hasegawa have overscaled the aircraft slightly but the question of why this should be is hard to answer. It all goes back, I suppose, to which set of dimensions the mold makers use. Check P-40 dimensions in several references and they always vary, indicating that kit manufacturers may just have a problem or two in this respect.

Older P-40 kits regularly reappear at model events, offered either in original boxed form (at quite high asking prices) or in bags without instruction sheets and consequently somewhat cheaper. More recently Russian and Eastern European manufacturers have revitalized the molds and the kits are once again being imported

into the UK. Newer P-40B kits in 1/72 scale have recently become available too.

As this book was being completed Revell brought out a short fuselage P-40K, a variant that had generally been overlooked by the industry. Another welcome addition to this scale, the kit has fine engraved surface detail, but as indicated previously, the mainwheels need replacing with something more in keeping with those of the original aircraft.

QUARTER-SCALE SUPERIORITY

Academy's P-40C, released in 2000, set new standards for the earliest of the first combat-worthy Warhawks, its restrained panel detail engraved into the plastic as it should be contrasting with the raised line approach long adopted by Monogram.

Molded in light gray plastic the Academy kit goes together very well and is one of many contemporary kits that fall easily into the "out of the box" building category. One curious but in my case welcome inclusion is a solid D/F loop fairing. No mention of this item is made on the instruction sheet and although manufacturers have been known to add additional parts and indeed whole extra sprues to kits that are to be part of a series, one D/F loop is a mystery. It may be that Academy are to re-tool the P-40C into a P-40K, a sub type that in some instances had this addition on the fuselage aft of the cockpit. I'm not complaining as the part came in very useful for just such a model, a P-40K of the 23d Fighter Group.

One other area that needs commenting on is Academy's slight "dumbing down" of the P-40C's internal detail. As it retained cowling guns the aircraft had the breeches flanking the instrument panel. These should be at least three separate parts. The gun rearming and inspection panels are among the few hinged items that may be incorporated onto a P-40C without turning the model into a diorama.

MORE P-40S REVIEWED

In recent years I've gone a little OTT for the Warhawk and built the Frog P-40B, the Hasegawa P-40N, two 1/48-scale AMT-ERTL kits, the Monogram Snap-Tite offering to an uncertain scale, converted the TP-40N from Monogram kits, dry run the Mauve P-40N and done enough work on the Revell 1/32 P-40E to note the great possibilities this kit offers for super detailing.

Within the above building program one of the AMT kits was finished as a P-40F using the AeroMaster conversion parts, and a P-40K, one of several options provided for in the AMT/ERTL Warhawk which is basically an "E" model but is sold with the P-40K's dorsal fin as an optional tail section. Forgive the many acronyms, but banging on about Warhawks and Kittyhawks would only confuse the issue, although I do appreciate that British readers might more readily identify the different P-40s using RAF nomenclature.

For a 1/48-scale P-40K, the AMT kit is a good starting point although the general fit of parts leaves something to be desired. Recessed panel lines make for an excellent restrained surface finish and overall the assembled kit looks very convincing providing that areas such as the wing dihedral can be achieved correctly. The kit also has a few anomalies such as fuselage location points for the cockpit sidewalls that do not have the corresponding pins. You locate the sidewall sections into the cockpit floor, which makes for rather weak assembly until the completed cockpit box is located into the fuselage halves. Even then, the panels are a little "off the walls."

Separate side panels containing the exhausts are provided to show an engine (no parts for which are provided) but the exhausts themselves do not duplicate the fishtail design of the original. Incorrect exhaust pipe shape is a common fault with numerous P-40 kits, unfortunately.

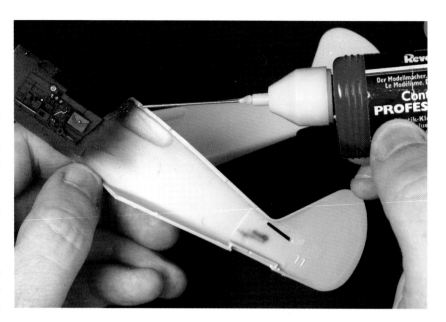

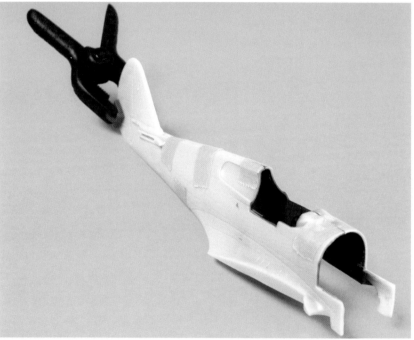

The AMT P-40K also includes a seat back panel that is incorrectly kinked to angle forwards. This is doubly odd as the corresponding item in the same company's P-40L/N kit is a correctly angled back, a straight piece of plastic containing the headrest being provided in that instance.

Persuading the AeroMaster P-40F nose to mate with a truncated AMT fuselage has its difficulties. AeroMaster actually recommend using the Mauve P-40N but as these kits are a bit hard to come by and I'd already set aside the single example I had, there was no choice but to seek an alternative if I wanted a P-40F in 1/48.

Carefully cut at the points suggested in the AeroMaster instruction sheet, the AMT kit will accept the new nose without too much

ABOVE TOP The next step for our P-40F: cementing. Some plastic cements have a needle applicator that makes precise placement a simple matter. Adhesive was run around each half of the P-40F's fuselage.

ABOVE The parts were then taped and clamped. The fuselage was set aside until the glue had thoroughly set.

RIGHT The bottom of the P-40F's resin replacement nose protrudes into the center of the wing. The area to be removed has been marked out, and a scriber is being used to accentuate the cut line.

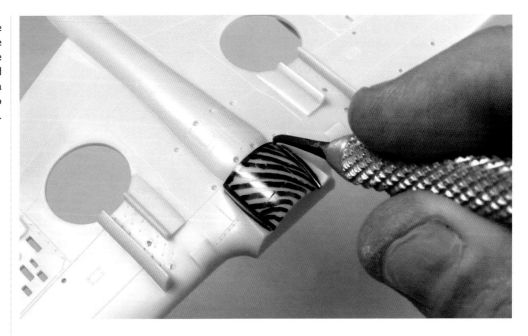

RIGHT A razor saw was once again used to remove this section.

OPPOSITE TOP The minor steps and ledges on the resin nose are dealt with by gluing small pieces of plastic card to strategic positions. These pieces of card force the plastic of the fuselage to line up with the contours of the resin nose. Several configurations were tested before the best result was found.

OPPOSITE MIDDLE Final fitting of the adjusted nose proved to be free of gaps, steps and ridges.

OPPOSITE BOTTOM The plastic and resin was blended by sanding.

difficulty – that tends to come with the rest of the kit! Although the component parts are well molded, numerous gaps will appear, particularly at the wing roots. As with some other kits in which the fuselage is set or "sprung" into the completed wing the dihedral angle can become excessive in an effort to close the gaps and the only remedy is to resort to Plasticard shims and filler.

The completed kit is one of those that may take a little getting used to: the Merlin engine did not exactly flatter the P-40's hitherto elegant nose profile and in this case a weighted nose due to density of the resin composition makes you momentarily wonder where the nosewheel went! Having said that, the P-40 and L were widely used by US combat groups and the kit opens up many markings possibilities that had previously to be neglected.

SNAP-TITE WARHAWK

On the subject of P-40Fs, I remembered a relevant oddity in my "yet to build" kit farm, namely a "Snap-Tite" Merlin-engine Warhawk, circa 1974. You may recall this Monogram sub-series, aimed firmly at the junior end of the market and maybe because of that, not adhering to standard scales. These kits seem largely to have been ignored by the serious modeler, which is a little short sighted to my mind as each one should really stand alone and not be judged in direct comparison with another. The Warhawk is larger than 1/72 and probably works out at about 1/64 – but the point is that it was the first P-40F to appear. It builds up well and if any comparison needs to be made, Monogram also released a P-51D as a Snap-Tite in the same scale. Also, Aurora once came up with an F4F Wildcat in much the same scale.

With the rider that the over-large anchorage points of this kind of "no glue" kit need trimming or removing, a model designed to be simple and quick to build has some undoubted advantages. By all means add construction strength with adhesive (as Monogram's instruction sheet suggests) and do remove the raised panel lines. This kit is probably worth the effort as to my knowledge no P-40Fs exist in scales smaller than 1/48 – but as the photos here show, that sub-type has been well recognised in the larger scale.

One drawback to an odd scale kit is the lack of correctly sized markings. But again I found that with the advantage of a bulging decal file, suitable national insignia could be found. Incidentally while searching to find something suitable I realized that the P-40 is among the few US fighters to have fuselage and wing national insignia to the same dimensions.

Talking of insignia, few modelers of the Warhawk will have failed to notice the commemorative, 15,000th P-40N with national markings of all the countries supplied by Curtiss. The Mauve kit has been updated and re-released by a Japanese company called Create 310, complete with all those markings.

P-47 THUNDERBOLT

Soon after it first entered service with the 8th Air Force, Republic's mighty P-47 was being weighed down with all manner of "things under wings." Drop tanks were followed by bombs, rocket tubes and HVARs, extras which manufacturers have not been slow to include as optional extras in their kits. Unfortunately, while concentrating on filling up the sprues with stores, they often appear to have overlooked the true outline shape of the old T-bolt and once again the 1/72-scale kits on offer have historically required crossing-kitting with components from others to build one good example. In particular, the addition of custom parts for Thunderbolts included such items as determining whether a given example was fitted with Hamilton or Curtiss propellers with standard or "paddle" blades.

In the case of some older models, there was the chore of constructing wheel well walls and in addition, detailing stores racks molded integrally as part of the lower wing, something that while not critical, could hamper the camouflage and markings process. Some of us will have cut our teeth on the ancient Frog razorback kit, which although ignored these days, was not the worst model of its type by any means – and it did seem to be the right size.

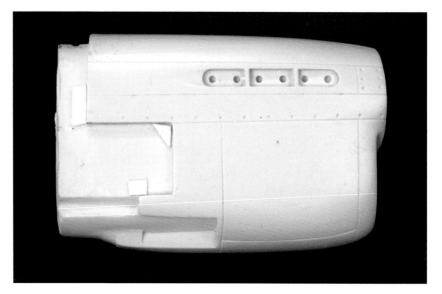

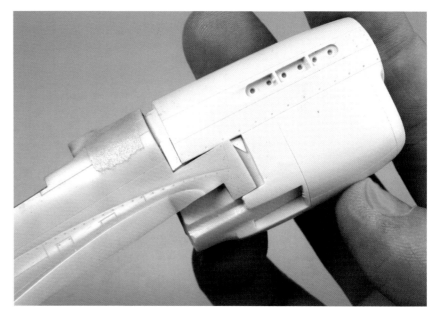

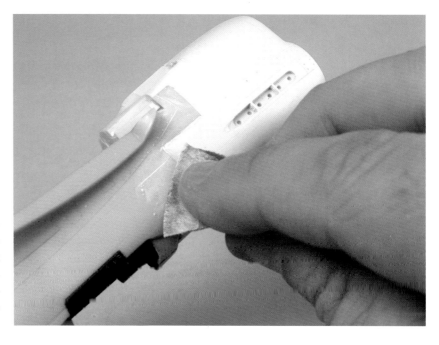

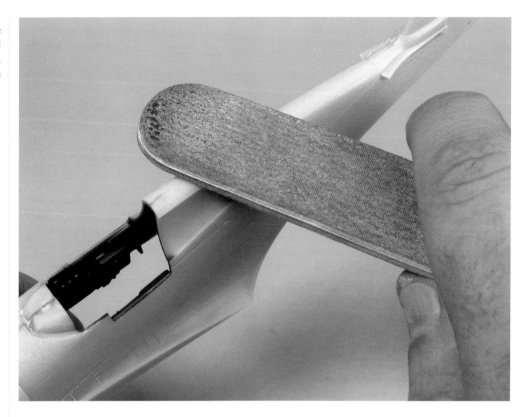

RIGHT The remaining fuselage seams on our P-40F were tidied up with a sanding stick. Later, they were smoothed with fine grade abrasive paper.

REPUBLIC P-47 IN 1/32

The razorback P-47 is also the subject of a Revell 1/32-scale kit, which requires suitable modification. More work is needed to turn the razorback into something acceptable as some fundamental airframe errors have crept into the moldings and these need to be attended to before other work is tackled. Not all these Revell kits extended to underwing stores – or even the racks – but the P-47 I used included a pair of racks with British-style bombs (some kits were marketed with RAF markings for an aircraft serving in Burma) and a suspicious looking centerline drop tank.

During the time period when these kits were originally available, I invested in a set of 1/32-scale vacuform drop tanks marketed by Horizon Conversions. By offering standard tanks for the P-47/P-51, the "flat" tank often seen on Thunderbolts, plus the very large ferry tanks for the P-38, this set is particularly useful. Armed with the Horizon drop tanks and any other items more recently made available for aircraft models in this scale, older kits may consequently be finished to look as they should. Latterly, some of the standard-pattern AAF fighter drop tanks have been replicated in 1/32-scale injection-molded kits, notably by the Hasegawa P-51D, which is adaptable to the P-47, but the P-38's underwing loads seems to have been rather overlooked in this respect.

Unfortunately the P-47 bubbletop version is beyond redemption as it comes out of the box because the high point of the sliding cockpit hood is not really present, this part seemingly being molded too short. The consequent "cut off" look is very noticeable and an alternative canopy will have to be found. But one can hardly leave out the P-47 in a collection of 1/32 scale American fighters and by carrying out corrective work, the Revell kit can be made to look very impressive indeed.

P-51

The modern day kit scene shows that the manufacturers are at long last aware that North American's finest came in several distinctly different guises. A look back at the releases of past decades proves that Monogram appreciated that there was a P-51B as well as the bubbletop D and duly released kits in 1/48 and 1/72 scales in 1967. The company only added a P-51D in the larger scale ten years later but in the meantime, its happy customers sat back and waited for the rest of the world to catch up. It did but slowly, in more ways than one.

It was 1995 before Tamiya added a P-51D to its excellent 1/48-scale range. The kit, which had a straightforward Mustang design approach, included teardrop external fuel tanks and separate flaps, plus nicely detailed wheel wells that were pressed as separate parts. Two cockpit canopies, one to represent an aircraft built at Inglewood and one at Dallas, were also provided. A neat touch on the four-aircraft subject decal sheet was the inclusion of an "aluminum" effect surround to the national insignia. This enabled the subject model, unimaginatively that well known P-51D coded E2-S of the 361st Fighter Group, to be completed with the masked off outline around the "stars and bars" not being compromised by awkward masking or a shaky handheld brush.

This and other P-51Ds of the 361st famously – or notoriously – wore tactical upper surface camouflage, which for years many people thought to have been insignia blue or even red. Only when one of a number of color photos taken of this aircraft and three others in a four ship formation was finally subjected to careful reproduction did we realize that the upper surface color had been olive drab all along.

While Tamiya thus demonstrated an admirable in-depth approach to decal research, it was not really needed for the fuselage of this particular machine, which had the OD tactical camouflage touching the national insignia at the top, without an NMF outline. It was however masked out when AEAF stripes were applied.

P-51 IN 1/32 SCALE

As the only kit of an early Merlin Mustang in 1/32 scale I had no choice but to use the Revell kit as a basis and carry out a little mixing and matching, primarily to add an engine of the right frontal cross-section. As it comes the kit has front end contours somewhere between an Allison and a Merlin but not exactly right for either. An engine section molded to the correct

dimensions can be cut from either a "solid" Monogram P-51D or the same company's "Phantom Mustang" that was also pressed in this scale.

I chose to use these older kits purely on the grounds of availability and the fact that the release of the Hasegawa P-51D quickly put them into the "spares only" category. While this may be an added reason to use either of the Monogram engines, they do not fit perfectly all round. I found a degree of fairing-in to be necessary on the undersides and the thin wing roots also require building up with filler. Anyone wishing to tackle this conversion would be better using the Hasegawa kit – which will in any event probably be the only Mustang available – as the engine apparently mates better with the Revell kit fuselage. Also, the spinner, propeller and mainwheels of the Japanese kit are much more accurate.

An early version Mustang in this scale has numerous markings possibilities, not to mention ordnance loads that will in some cases have to be scratch built. Bombs should be no problem as numerous kits supply these in abundance, even though they may not necessarily be to 1/32 scale. A large size bomb in a 1/48 scale bomber kit can usually double for a smaller size on a fighter in the larger scale – i.e. a 1/48 scale 1,000 pounder can become a 500 pounder in 1/32 scale, and so forth. Customizing plastic rod can be used to manufacture a pair of M10 rocket launchers for the P-51B/C.

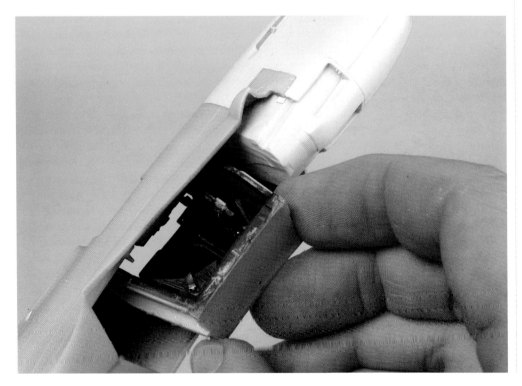

LEFT The P-40F's cockpit tub was next inserted into the fuselage. The fit was extremely precise, with the assembly clicking in place without the benefit of glue. A bead of superglue was added to the back of the pilot's bulkhead and along the bottom edges of the cockpit floor to ensure it did not come loose later.

Without its engine the truncated Hasegawa P-51D could form the basis for a super-detailed diorama where the building work concentrates on what goes on at the front end, but below the skin. Start by inserting a Plasticard firewall at the point the engine has been cut off to use on the P-51B, drill this to take various ancillaries and work slowly forward from there. The spares box will provide many of the necessary bits and pieces and when the engine is installed, the discarded sections of the Revell P-51B might be adapted for display as separate panels. The fact that these are slightly undersized won't really be noticed provided that they are sanded down and painted.

Finally, the thought occurs that one could add the uncowled, detailed Merlin engine to the Revell P-51B and not bother with cutting up the Hasegawa kit but this would still leave the slight challenge of modifying the propeller blades and adding new tires of the correct cross-section. Then again, the contours of the original Revell kit nose might, just might, be adaptable to an Allison although this would involve a considerable amount of work.

EARLY MUSTANG MODELS

Manifestation of an early Mustang in plastic kit form to 1/48 scale occurred in the early 1990s when the US company Accurate Miniatures released not one but three Allison-engine P-51s: a P-51 (with no suffix letter), a P-51A and an A-36. This brave "go for broke" approach was a gamble that the market had vastly increased in sophistication and indeed knowledge through acquiring the many fine references that have appeared in recent years. It worked. AM achieved sales good enough to keep the company going so that currently it is branching out into other subjects and gaining an enviable reputation for quality. The going has reportedly been hard at times, but to date AM's stable of early Allison-engine Mustangs has been joined by a P-51B and P-51C, both of which are welcome replacements or adjuncts to the still useful Monogram kit in this scale. More recent still is a Tamiya release of a P-51B, which, if previous kits are anything to go by, will be little short of highly desirable.

There is though a downside to all these new releases in that the modeler may prefer to build a stable of Mustangs from the same kit. It all boils down, I suppose, not only to what is preferred but availability. While some areas of the world stock enough plastic kits to cater for all tastes at all times, this is not always the case. An impulse buy may result in essentially the same kit but with a slight contrast, particularly

in surface finish and a different end result. Therefore if you wish to build representative P-51Bs of the entire 8th Fighter Command it may be worth investing in several kits at once. Which one is entirely at the modeler's discretion, of course.

In 1/72 scale the Mustang situation was, as ever, that much gloomier than in 1/48: of them all only Frog was once bold enough to kit an injection molded A-36. Unlike the reasonable early P-40B from this manufacturer, the Apache represented another lost opportunity to corner a hungry slice of the market, as the kit suffered from some major errors. Instead of carefully designing a model that could have led to numerous conversion possibilities to create several of the Allison-engine Mustangs, the modeler was obliged to wield scalpel, knife and sandpaper to create what it said on the box top in the first place.

At long last Condor (MPC) with a new A-36 has plugged this gap in the kit line-up of early Mustang variants in this scale. Having not seen a copy as yet, I cannot say whether it hits the mark in regard to outline accuracy.

Among the accessory/conversion sets for P-51s that from Verlinden Productions provides a full range of underwing stores for a 1/48-scale P-51D. One of the most useful additions, it is well worth obtaining, not because it introduces much that is new but by including a range of P-51 rocket, bomb and drop tank sections to very accurate tolerances. This is also one of the few accessory sets that recognizes the difference between the early and later style of main wing racks designed for the carriage of drop tanks or bombs on the P-51B. Broadly speaking these had the carrier crutches mounted either at the top – flush with the wing – on earlier style racks and on the lower edge on the racks fitted to P-51Ds and Ks.

By combining resin and photo-etch parts this particular accessory kit enables the modeler to apply scale fins to bombs and "straps" around HVARs and drop tanks: both were small enough on the full-sized aircraft and they come out (or they should) as positively minute when scaled down. Verlinden's set also includes the sway braces for field modifications of racks, plus a full set of rockets for the triple M-10 bazooka tubes.

Photographs indicate that several methods were used to locate ordnance and fuel tanks safely under P-51 wings, particularly in the CBI, where some P-51Bs and Cs actually carried two drop tanks under each wing, heavily braced to keep them in place. In a theater denied almost everything for long periods of time, the

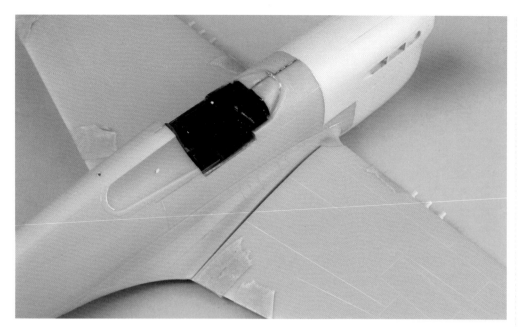

LEFT Test-fitting the wing assembly on the P-40F seemed to confirm this kit's reputation for an ill-fitting wing root. However, this problem has a very simple solution.

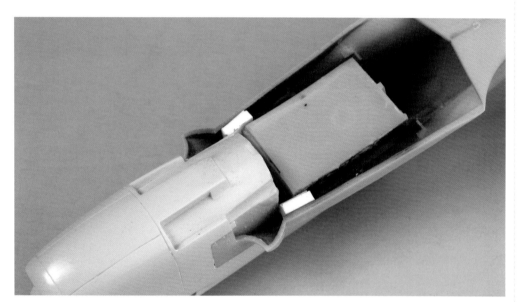

LEFT Wedges of plastic were inserted between the cockpit floor and the fuselage wing root to increase the width of the fuselage where it meets the wing.

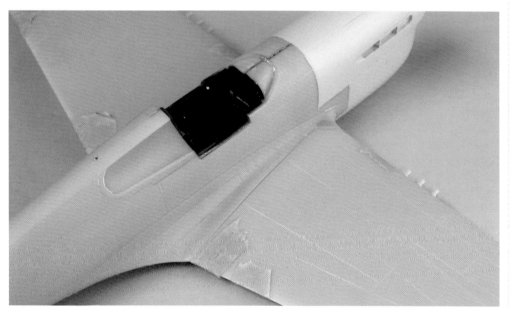

LEFT The wing root gap was closed without using putty after a few minutes adjusting the plastic wedges. Note that the wings are not even glued to the fuselage in this photo.

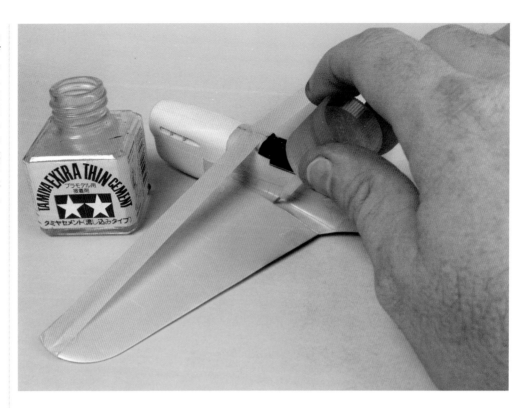

RIGHT With the P-40F's fuselage spread, the dihedral of the wing was a little flat. To address this problem, Tamiya masking tape was attached underneath one wing tip and stretched across the top of the model to the other wingtip. This had the dual effect of restoring the correct dihedral and squeezing an even tighter fit at the wing roots.

squadrons were obliged to jury-rig their own bomb shackles before the regular items were hauled over the Hump route from India. And although the European-based air forces generally had a good supply of standardized equipment for their Mustangs, variations may still be found abroad.

The type of accessory kit produced by Verlinden is invaluable for ringing the changes and improving still further the components provided in kits. Other sets, intended for detailing P-47 and P-38 kits, are available in the range.

NORTHROP P-61

A purely personal view of the P-61 is that it looks far better with its top turret in place than without. Most modelers did not of course ever have to put up with the blast of four "fifties" just above their heads, or experience the buffeting that sometimes resulted when the turreted aircraft was flung around the night skies of Europe or the Pacific. That led to the majority of the 9th Air Force P-61s operating without the turret, which certainly altered its dramatic lines. Turrets were actually re-introduced onto P-61s operating in the ETO at the end of the war, so all is not lost for the modeler seeking such a combination of configuration and markings.

A mighty beast of an airplane, the "Widow" has a no-nonsense look that makes it an ideal kit subject. This is particularly so in a larger scale, as Monogram proved very well indeed by offering a superb kit that incorporated both

the "short nosed" P-61A and "long nosed" P-61B; either version can be an eye-catching centerpiece of any display.

Again the kits in 1/72 disappointed, those by Frog and Airfix indicating a very different approach to the same subject. Frog, whilst achieving an acceptable top fuselage contour (no turret was included) gave its P-61 odd, cross-hatch surface detail meant presumably to represent rivets, and messed up the dimensions of the fuselage, not to mention the rear glazed section. Frog's UK counterpart covered the black airframe in "trademark" rivets but added an admirable degree of detail such as separate wing spoilers, an alternative top turret, drop tanks and so forth. Unfortunately the top line of the fuselage, including the cockpit profile, was far too square with pronounced corners. Re-profiling was a difficult option as the cockpit canopy also had sharp corners that could not really be adapted without a remolding job. That said, the Airfix kit is one to use as a starting point if an older P-61 kit is required in this scale, with perhaps some cross-kitting using the Frog offering's best bits.

Alternatively the modeler can splash out on a completely new kit such as that released by the Dragon or Revell concerns.

DOUGLAS P-70

If your favored model scale is 1/48, the regular addition of kits to this size in recent years has been very satisfying indeed. The current situation is that there are now very few gaps in the ranks of US Army fighter models, and in this scale at least, the majority of them are satisfyingly accurate. The appearance of the AMT A-20 raised the possibility of conversion into a P-70 night fighter, a type that could have taken a prize as one of the least known US combat aircraft of World War 2 until a few years ago.

While not marketed as a P-70 per se, the 1/48 AMT A-20J followed an excellent vacuform Koster Aviation Enterprises kit in this scale, which also featured two dorsal turret variants. I understand, however, that conversion sets are available to turn this or the AMT Havoc into the earlier version, forming the basis for the first US night fighter.

In 1/72 scale, the old Revell kit of 1975 vintage was actually marketed as a P-70, an update of the company's earlier release as a standard Boston. Included in the night fighter version was a solid nose section, under fuselage cannon tray and radar aerials. Pressed in black plastic, it remains the best of the early model A-20/Bostons available in this scale, those by Airfix and Frog having their share of outline faults. Long after the two latter kits had all but disappeared, Matchbox released an A-20G/J: having fuselage sections incorporating the rear dorsal turret was welcome, although the overly large engine cowlings demanded replacement with something more in scale – the 1/72 cross-kitting saga continued. In any event, all P-70s that saw action had the early-style rear gun position with sliding transparent panels, as incorporated on most Boston/Havoc models.

In conclusion, a word or two about kits of the "foreigners," both the fighters of other nations that wore US insignia and those nationals who flew US aircraft but applied their own national insignia as well as the "stars and bars." They became an important part of inventory in the ETO, MTO and the Pacific.

SUPERMARINE SPITFIRE

Among the non-American aircraft serving the USAAF in a wartime fighter role, the Supermarine Spitfire was the most numerous and important from the earliest days of the conflict. From being the mount of individual pilots who joined RAF units, through the three Eagle Squadrons in 1941-42 to flying long range PR sorties for the 8th Air Force, Spitfires served when nothing comparable was available. Operating in the Mediterranean with the equipment starved 12th Air Force when it was desperate for aircraft to support Operation Torch,k the Spitfire squadrons of the 31st and 52d Fighter Groups were well to the fore. A

type that wore a fascinating variety of markings from large size renderings of Old Glory (so that Vichy French forces would recognize it during the early days of Torch) to NMF aircraft wearing full stars and bars and double code letters, the Spit was an enduring favorite among many US pilots.

In 1/48 scale, kits from Otaki and Airfix (now one and the same as regards most of the former company's fighters) are among the legion of Spitfire models, although there are fewer in this scale than the smaller ones. Otaki's original Spitfire was pressed as a Mk VIII, making it ideal for a 12th Air Force machine. Under its own banner Airfix released a good Mk V, the version very widely used by the Americans, both in the UK and MTO. Quarter-scale Mk IXs were relatively thin on the ground after Monogram produced the first one to be generally available in the 1960s, although the situation has since been redressed by a number of new kits, not to mention resin accessories intended for use with Mk Vs to make the necessary changes and updates.

Not surprisingly a plethora of Spitfires have appeared from UK manufacturers in 1/72 scale, with the seemingly inevitable variation in accuracy. They have been joined by a number of offerings from France, the Czech Republic and Poland, proof positive that such a perennially favorite subject will continue to be added to the world's kit lists.

As with other types, the Spitfire has taken years to grow in accuracy as a plastic kit and this writer would recommend looking for the most recent kits rather than hack older ones about. Astute modelers familiar with the aircraft will look in particular at any kit's wing underside to check how well the subtle "gull wing" effect has been reproduced. This may not be a personal issue if the rest of the kit seems good enough (the latest Revell Mk V is a case in point – it has almost flat wing undersides but is otherwise a fine little kit) but the full size contours really should be at least indicated, I feel.

Current Spitfire kits don't need the degree of cross fertilization *de rigueur* in decades past and the 21st century modeler has far more references, particularly color photographs, that were unavailable even 20 years after the plastic modeling hobby secured a niche in the commercial market place.

Moving up to the larger scales, both Revell and Hasegawa produced early (Mks I to V) Merlin Spitfires in 1/32 scale as did Airfix in 1/24 scale. Of these I have previously built the Hasegawa kit to produce an Eagle Squadron

Mk V. The kit is superb, offering all the major variations on the Mk V theme in regard to tropical filters, different size radiators, and a choice of standard or clipped wings as well as a choice of standard and bullet proof windscreens. Once completed it surprised me to realize after not a few years of abstinence (at least in building Spits) just how big an aircraft it is compared to a P-51 in the same scale.

Although the Hasegawa kit is very impressive, despite some hard to disguise sink marks along the wings, the fit of parts on my example also left a little to be desired, probably due to long-term storage. Also, the wing sub-assemblies are substantial pieces of plastic which have to be persuaded to mate without moving out of alignment. The excellent cockpit sub-assembly, which is almost a model in its own right.

The method of splicing Plasticard strip into the gaps was particularly successful on the Spit as the lower wing half which incorporated those long, sweeping characteristic wing fillets, is in one piece. Once the top wing halves are joined this sub assembly is quite weighty and it must be persuaded to fair smoothly into the fuselage with only thin plastic ridges to anchor it firmly. By inserting plastic strip fore and aft along one fillet and across the rear joint, the job was completed satisfactorily with no need for filler.

Markings for the Spitfire V of No. 121 Squadron (latterly the 336th FS of the 4th Fighter Group) posed a problem at first. Without any custom decals to hand I resorted to an "old three into one" HisAirDec sheet of US national insignia. With the drawback that the finished decal is thicker than one would expect in today's kits, this method nevertheless served its purpose. The yellow ring, blue background and white star combination creates some "strike-through" but in this case it didn't matter. The majority of Eagle Squadron Spits were "hand me downs" that invariably had their RAF roundels overpainted with the US marking.

For the codes I chose relatively "easy" letters that were masked with strips of Post-It and sprayed in Sky, the rear fuselage band being similarly treated. Eagle Squadron Spitfire Vs came with the detail differences applicable to the mark, the most obvious being full span and clipped wingtips and standard or external bullet-proof windscreens. In regard to markings there was sprinkling of personal decoration, which included the "double eagle" emblem on certain individual aircraft, but only a handful of serial numbers can definitely be tied in with codes. As the serial digits were not always painted on the rear fuselage the problem of definite identification remains conjectural in some cases. Equally, Spitfires also show evidence of overpainted serials, part serials and a general lack of fin flashes, as per American practice. Many individual machines had seen a fair degree of service before being passed to the Eagles, so a weathered appearance is quite in order on a representative model. Other USAAF Spitfires operated extensively in the Mediterranean and the many kits of the Mk V, VII and IX may be finished in appropriate markings.

HAWKER HURRICANE

Although used by all three Eagle Squadrons, the Hurricane Mks I and II did not remain in service long enough for any examples to adopt USAAF star insignia. So even though a collection of American-operated fighters could legitimately include one or two Eagle Hurricanes, they will seem at first glance to be RAF machines. But all is not lost. During Operation Torch, carrier borne Canadian-built Sea Hurricane XIIs did have the "universal" white star marking carried by all aircraft likely to be operating over that area of North Africa and come in contact with hostile Vichy French forces. These particular Hurris with their yellow outlined fuselage insignia would therefore be more in keeping with a collection of AAF fighters.

Which kit to chose for an American-manned Hurricane is a moot point: in 1/72 scale Hasegawa currently puts out a neat Mk II and there are several survivors of a long line that has included, apart from the more familiar labels of Airfix and Revell, a rare venture into plastic by Keil Kraft, a company previously known primarily for flying scale models in wood. This latter kit was a bit on the heavy side but it had nice detail and was no worse than its contemporaries.

There are several good 1/48-scale Hurricanes on the market and although none are, to the writer's knowledge, labeled as a (hooked) Sea Hurricane Mk XII, the sub-type that was the equivalent of the Mk IIC. Again though I would offer an opinion that Monogram does as good a job as any in this scale. The company's convertible kit gave options to build the Mk II, IV and a tropicalized Mk Vc version but there was no provision for a "hooked" aircraft. This addition is relatively simple to make in conjunction with a study of Hurricane references. You will of course have to modify the fuselage undersides to take a tail hook and its "V" struts. There are plenty of scale drawings to help with the dimensions.

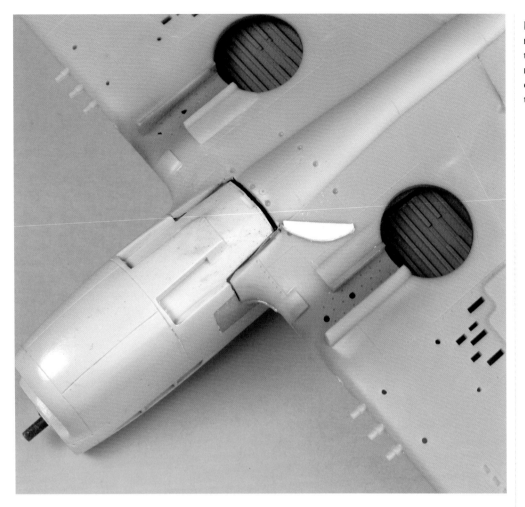

LEFT I removed too much material from the lower wing of the P-40F where it met the nose, so a scrap of styrene was cut to the approximate shape of the gap.

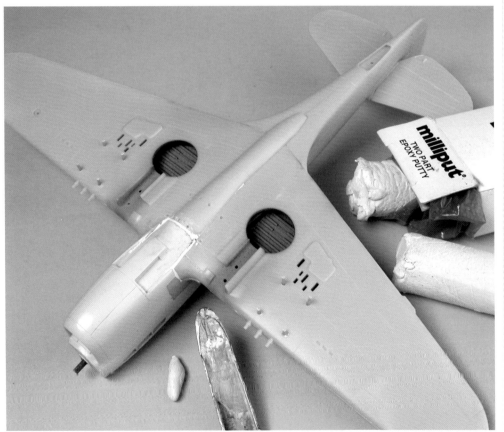

LEFT After the gap was plugged by gluing the styrene in place, it was trimmed then filled with Milliput two-part epoxy putty. A tiny ball from each stick was mixed together to prepare the putty for use. It was applied with my favorite putty trowel – an old staple remover!

BRISTOL BEAUFIGHTER

A type quite widely used but hardly loved by the USAAF, the Beaufighter was a stop gap twin that served pending the delivery of the P-61. The trouble was that most of the pilots who were destined to fly the Beau operationally in the MTO had trained on the P-70 – going back to a tail dragger was seen as a retrograde step. With the benefit of hindsight we can well understand their views. Added to an unfamiliar ground angle was the fact that the Beau had engines with enough torque to put a Spitfire to shame and send the Bristol twin careering off the runway. It nevertheless helped the crews to get their eye in over the Western Desert and Italy before the Widow (and a few Mosquitos) came along at the eleventh hour to re-equip the squadrons based in the Mediterranean.

The Tamiya kit broke the seeming embargo on any Beaufighter kit being produced in 1/48 scale, a situation that had prevailed for years. An excellent kit well up to modern tooling and molding standards, the Japanese release may be built as a USAAF-operated Beau Mk VI or X,

with or without the thimble nose radome, which is supplied.

In 1/72 scale, Airfix again had the field to itself with a Beau Mk X released in the 1960s. A Frog kit came later with some minor improvements but modelers had another lengthy wait for anything better, a gap that was filled by Hasegawa only as recently as 2001.

Long before that, Revell ploughed on with new additions to their larger scale fighter range by producing a Beaufighter Mk I in 1/32 scale during the course of the 1970s.

A great expanse of black plastic parts, this kit lacked the internal detail modelers had come to expect in this scale although its outline and components were basically accurate. That was the trouble with this entire range – basic was usually the operative word and anyone wishing to upgrade the variant (a straight tail Mk I as originally released) faced a heap of work. Converting the model into a night fighter as used by the USAAF is however not an insurmountable task. It can involve adapting the kit's horizontal tailplane into a dihedral

unit, changing the nose contours to accept a centrimetric radar scanner and improving the clear bubble over the observer's position to incorporate a machine gun. Alternatively an early straight tailed Mk VI might be found, the AAF accepting a variety of Beau sub-types.

END NOTE

Using the word "advanced" is a minefield in modeling because what is a difficult task to one person will seem to be routine to another. But having been a sucker for American fighter kits for as long as I can remember, I've also kicked the "strictly all one scale" viewpoint. As kits grew ever more sophisticated I was attracted to try other sizes, the upshot being that now I'll add a good Mustang, Thunderbolt, Warhawk or whatever, to my collection irrespective of the scale. This is no great revelation in that it means that I now opt primarily for 1/48 scale but like the added possibilities with 1/32 scale. Another drawback of being too partisan for one comparative size is that one can miss the far superior releases outside the preferred favorite scale. Change your habit though and you'll likely be scrabbling to find the fine kits you

missed in this new scale first time around. Not that this is a great problem: molds for plastic kits are expensive and they rarely seem to be melted down or whatever they do with them. Providing that you can be patient, someone will eventually re-release that overlooked model subject, probably at a much better price that those asked by specialist suppliers for "original" kits that have rocketed in price. There is also a distinct possibility that someone will kit the subject better than the original you spent time trying to track down.

ABOVE The extra effort spent preparing the P-40F's parts was worthwhile, as it saved a lot of time fixing alignment and gap problems later. The resin cockpit from Cutting Edge Modelworks was also a good investment due to its high level of visibility under that big, open canopy. Note that the techniques for achieving the P-40F's finish will be dealt with in the following chapter.

CHAPTER 6
SPECIAL TECHNIQUES

CAMOUFLAGE & COLORING

Camouflage is a word that has become synonymous in aviation terms with two or more colors applied to an airframe in a disruptive pattern. Such was adopted almost universally by the RAF as "shadow shading" of its combat aircraft, but in World War 2 no such scheme was specified for US aircraft despite a series of pre-war tests. Extensive painting of fighters in a variety of experimental patterns led to the conclusion that none of these quite elaborate schemes would be adopted. Instead, a simple overall top surface coat of Olive Drab with Neutral Gray on the undersides would suffice. As all camouflage paint is to some extent compromised by the application of national insignia and other identity markings, it was felt that this American scheme was vastly superior to a bright natural metal finish. (See the accompanying images on pages 99–106 for more details on recreating this scheme.)

While the majority of USAAF fighters consequently saw action in these regulation colors, many examples left the factories in approximations of British shadow shading

patterns. There were numerous variations of outline and differences in color shades, owing to the fact that American paints were generally used to apply the colors. The matching process inevitably came close only on occasion.

In unit service, when aircraft such as the P-39 and P-40 were diverted from British contracts, the colors were subjected to extreme temperatures, high humidity levels and generally rugged conditions when they were deployed in the Pacific or the Mediterranean. Some colors took on strange hues that almost defy accurate identification from paint charts all these years on.

Numerous Warhawks and Airacobras were given dark green and brown camouflage at their respective factories or modification centers, the exact shades often being broadly interpreted. In service, such aircraft often appear to sport a shade of green seemingly closer to one of the US Olive Drab mixes rather than RAF Dark Green. Similar variations occur with Dark Earth and the underside color, which ranged from light blue (known as Duck Egg Green or Blue) to light gray and the infamous Sky Type "S", the latter being subject to rather broad

RIGHT US Army Air Force fighter aircraft displayed a wide variety of schemes. There are an even wider variety of techniques for depicting these color schemes. Three of these techniques are outlined in the images in this chapter – painting a natural metal finish, pre-shading, and post-shading. Firstly, the natural metal finish. This can be one of the most impressive ways to display your model aircraft, but the shiny metallic surface can be very unforgiving. Any scratches and other imperfections will be magnified, and some metallic paints will reward the lightest touch with a large fingerprint on the paintwork. Even so, a reliable and successful natural metal finish can be achieved.

interpretation. See the images on pages 107–113 for further guidance on reproducing the green and brown camouflage effect.

Among the reasons why many US fighter colors do not seem to conform to known paint specifications are (1) the result of exposure to harsh atmospheric conditions at the time; (2) the reference source being on color photographic stock that is more than 50 years old; and (3) the vagaries of the printing process. These are the main factors that play a part in distorting the model maker's perception of the true color actually applied to aircraft at factories and depots.

But among model makers, there is an ongoing need to know what the actual colors were. Much research has been undertaken to provide the answer and over the years model paint suppliers have wrestled with the problem. That they have largely succeeded is reflected in the ever growing range of enamel and acrylic paints intended specifically for models.

NATURAL METAL FINISH

When the USAAF generally dropped camouflage paint for military aircraft in 1943, the basic overall look of first-line fighters was radically altered. Type recognition markings and code letters were changed from white or other light color to black and for a short period the overall effect was quite plain, even dull. The general adoption of color trim for recognition purposes was made during 1944 particularly on fighters based in the ETO and MTO.

The basic construction of aircraft during World War 2 comprised a mixture of Alclad, dural, aluminum, titanium and magnesium. These materials, shaped into airframe panels, naturally enough exhibited slightly different tonal values which show up in photographs. Even aircraft built by sub contractors had areas of their airframes that were common to the type. A prime example was the darker panels running above and below behind the exhaust stubs on both sides of the P-51's cowling. These are always visible on NMF aircraft and should be indicated on any model. Tips and advice on how to achieve a top-quality NMF finish on your model are provided in the images on pages 92–98.

WEATHERING

An airbrush is clearly the optimum tool for applying weathering effects on models although various types of paint may also be applied by the stipple and dry brush technique; other marking media including graphite, felt tip or crayon may be applied using a soft cloth as an applicator. As a general rule, most aircraft irrespective of whether or not they start out with a matt or glossy paint finish or a "natural" surface finish, suffer a degree of weather effects once they start flying. The air is a hostile environment, bringing with it extreme heat and cold, with rain and humidity to effect the finish of airplanes that plough through it. This usually manifests itself in the form of discoloration and fading of the paintwork but the most common effect is that of buffing the surface to a shiny (or shinier) finish than it started out with. Added to that were the results of the regular removing and replacing of certain panels under general servicing, leading to chipping of painted edges, and the adverse effects on finish as a result of oil and fuel spillage.

Weathering additionally manifests itself in the form of exhaust staining and discoloration in specific areas. A light gray or beige colored streaking or faded effect indicated that an engine using leaded gasoline (petrol) was set to run at a lean, more or less correct throttle setting, while a darker color meant a richer fuel and air mixture, the variation being similar in principle to the various types of coloration visible on the inside of vehicle exhaust pipes.

Such effects are easier to achieve if they are applied, for example, in water paint over an enamel base coat. Gouache, which comes in a tube, is ideal for this purpose as it has a matt finish. Water soluble paint has the one big advantage in that it can be wiped off for repeat attempts, should the first application not result in quite what is required. This trouble-free method should stand up to a degree of heavy handed errors – thin paint, spillage and other troubles – without spoiling a good base surface. But familiarity with your airbrush (and perhaps its limitations) should eventually result in the correct degree of exhaust stains, grime and fading you are aiming at.

Pristine paintwork was a very low priority to men fighting for their lives, bombed by the enemy, racked by disease and under attack from a host of things that crawled, bit and stung. Modelers really need to crack those faded shades if they are to celebrate accurately the aircraft flown by those who fought in those desperate, valiant days in far flung theaters of war. Models of wartime aircraft should naturally reflect the wear and tear of front-line operations.

An interesting surface coloring can be achieved by varying the paint tones if the subject is in NMF but is a little more demanding if the

RIGHT This P-47D will wear a natural metal finish and invasion stripes on the lower surface of the fuselage. The first step was to paint the lower-mid section of the fuselage white, ensuring that this coat covered it thoroughly. Tamiya paints were used for the black and white invasion stripes.

RIGHT Tamiya masking tape was used to mask off the areas that were destined to stay white. Narrow strips of masking tape were first applied to the edges of the stripe. These narrow strips are required due to the compound curves and openings on the lower fuselage. A wide, single length of tape would most likely have wrinkles and gaps. A wider strip of tape is used to cover the gap between the two narrow borders of the stripe.

Note that a small blob of Blu-Tack has been stuffed into the supercharger vent, which was painted and weathered before assembly of the fuselage.

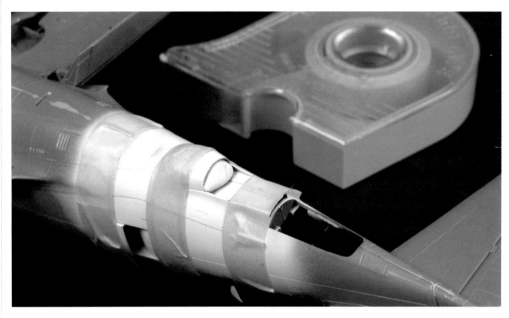

RIGHT Tamiya Acrylic Flat Black was sprayed in light coats. The Testor Aztek A470 airbrush used to paint this model can be seen in the background.

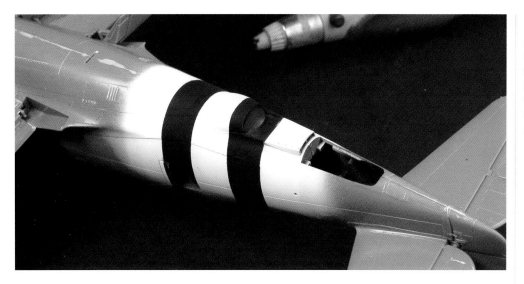

LEFT With the masking tape removed, the black and white stripes were revealed. Some adjustment to the width of the black stripes was required. The masking process was repeated until a satisfactory result was achieved.

model is to depict an OD and Gray machine. This is where the references again come to the rescue as each US fighter had areas of wear and fade common to all theaters. Different degrees of weathering can also be perceived on aircraft serving in Europe and the Pacific, a fact that reflected the extent of ground support and facilities.

Some fighter group commanders were fastidious about having smart aircraft on their flight line. Crew chiefs would have exhaust burns cleaned off aircraft after reckless young pilots had returned from missions and messed them up in the process. Other COs were not so particular: if the unit commander turned a blind eye to such things, more weathered aircraft might appear on the flight line. In the 8th Air Force in England, for whatever reason, the 339th Fighter Group seems to have flown scruffier Mustangs than, say, the 352d Fighter Group in the same county.

But despite all this, how often does one see a model with all markings in place flown by a 50-mission-plus pilot without a scratch or some evidence of exhaust staining? A finish as pristine as the day the aircraft was rolled out of the factory paint shop makes little sense to my way of thinking. I do know that there is a widespread belief that weathering an otherwise finished model runs the risk of ruining it, but if care is exercised, the problem should be overcome easily.

RUBBING DOWN RIVETS

On larger scale kits such as the Revell 1/32-scale P-38 and P-47 that are to be finished in camouflage paint, the notorious rivet heads can be lightly rubbed down before applying a first coat of olive drab. Rub the rivets down again and apply a second coat of paint. With the rivets still proud of the surface plastic, rub

them down for a third time, which should still have them visible through the paint. On some very weathered aircraft finishes, some rivet and panel detail should be seen, but not nearly to the extent visible on the kit when it is new. As a final touch, more OD can be sprayed over those areas not so prone to the wear and tear of operational flying. A patchy finish so typical of many first line aircraft should result.

The above rivet retention method obviously works best when the plastic base color is light gray or "natural plastic" rather than say, black or green, one reason why I – and I suspect many others – much prefer kits molded in a neutral shade.

But even if a kit is molded in darker color, this can provide contrast as the "rub down afterwards" method can be used if a weathered natural metal finish is chosen. One important

BELOW The entire area of black and white invasion stripes was finally masked in preparation for the natural metal finish. Tissue paper was dampened and pressed gently into the main wheel wells. This acts as a malleable mask for cavities that are otherwise hard to plug.

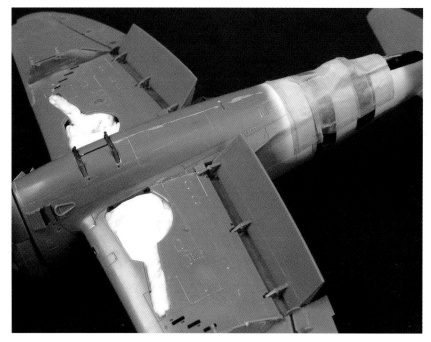

RIGHT Tamiya AS-12 Airframe Silver is only available in a spray can. This is a great shade for natural metal aircraft – neither too shiny nor too dull. The finish is also quite tough and durable, unlike some other natural metal paints. The only problem with this color is that the spray can sometimes produces a slight orange-peel texture on the surface of the paint. To avoid this problem, the contents of the can were emptied into a small disposable container. The container was covered with plastic wrap, a small hole was made in the plastic and the paint was sprayed into the hole. The result is a pool of silver lacquer in the bottom of the container that can be poured into a glass paint jar. If you are storing the decanted paint, do not tighten the cap too much as there may still be propellant in the paint, resulting in a possible build up of pressure in the jar. The silver lacquer was then sprayed over the entire model using the airbrush, resulting in a smooth, hard base coat.

point to remember here is to obtain a good coverage of paint before attempting to rub down. Above all, remember that you're trying to dirty up the finish, not ruin the paint finish you have already applied. I know that some modelers feel they are treading a very fine line when doing this and the answer is obviously to practice on an old kit first. A degree of boldness may also be in order!

Rubbing paintwork down seems to be more of an art than it might at first appear. I find that it is however one of the more pleasing aspects of modeling as the effect one creates will be unique to the individual model (and modeler). The trick is as ever, to keep the wear and tear within the confines of the visible effects of weathering on the full size airframe.

Even if the available photos of your subject aircraft do not show that much weathering on say, the wing root areas, another photo of a similar sub type assigned to the same squadron in the same theater may do so. "Borrowing" a bit more weathering to boost the final look of a model is I believe, quite legitimate. What you are then depicting is a typical finish for the theater of operations, which few can argue with.

DECALS & MARKINGS

While decals are currently reaching very high standards of accuracy and reproduction, I personally exercise a little caution in their application. While not in any way denying that decals are an integral part of modeling, they are sometimes used in my opinion to the detriment of the direct application method using suitable masks or stencils or indeed hand painting.

Looking closely at decals, one occasionally finds discrepancies between the panel lines on the full size aircraft and the width or depth of the decal. There can be certain limitations with the artwork/printing process and perhaps even the accuracy of scaling. Decal sheets are usually prepared from large size artwork or computer generated images and reduced to the required dimensions, and I've found instances where for example the aircraft serial numbers in 1/48 scale do not match those on the kit sheet because they are slightly too large. I found this out when trying to squeeze six digits onto the fin of a P-47 in this scale in the standard location between the leading edge and the rudder hinge line. A company that should know better had actually scaled all the numbers wrongly. I found there was little or no space at each end of the serial when applied to the model, when such is quite obvious in the reference.

In short, nobody should be overawed by the reputation of decal companies with voluminous lists, as they may miss certain details. I'm not implying that there is, in the hard commercial world, a race for quantity over quality. But one could state with some accuracy that there is a perceived desire to be first with decals for an exciting, eagerly awaited new kit. If the race is won by a poor product then the whole exercise is a waste of time. It must surely be preferable to hold back, get the various elements as accurate as possible, scale the sheet correctly and release it only when quality control is satisfied.

In defense of the commercial decal firms, however, there is the slight problem that some sheets are designed around specific kits. If this advisory small print is ignored or overlooked, applying the decals to an alternative kit can lead to problems. So be warned – even if all P-51s in a comparable scale appear to have the same vertical tail area, applying decals will show that it isn't necessarily so.

Painting markings straight onto the surface of the model must in some instances be superior to using a decal, which will invariably require very close cutting to eliminate all traces of the carrier film that surrounds every item on a waterslide sheet. The larger the decal, the more acute this problem can become. Things might get unwieldy with the decal demanding buckets of softening agent to persuade it to lay down on compound curves – and I have noted that in one or two instances this stuff will not only stain a light finish and "lift" the surface paint but it can fade detail off the decal as well. Hand painting may therefore produce superior results, particularly in 1/32 scale where acres of plastic provide ample scope for dispensing with the larger ones at least.

The US star or star-and-bar insignia tended to weather very well, even on a battered background, so the fact that model decals offer a high visibility, fairly clean appearance is quite in keeping with some subject aircraft. An exception would be those quite numerous instances where the insignia was deliberately dulled down on the grounds of reducing visibility.

To confuse this issue, some photos will appear to indicate a glossy application of the national insignia against a matt overall color scheme. It was not of course unknown for decals to be used for some aircraft markings, so check those references closely.

This question of glossy or matt model decals is a moot one as some photos definitely show reflections off what is known to be very matt surface. In general however a sheen affect, not necessarily uniform over all surfaces, should be aimed at. If necessary, one of the commercial matt or gloss varnishes can be applied to produce a uniform surface over the entire airframe.

While you are studying photo references, scrutinize the outline of code letters and

numbers. Dead straight edges and absolute vertical alignment was often the exception, wobbly outlines being very apparent on many aircraft. Identification digits on wartime aircraft leaned over, did not follow standard patterns, were presented overlarge or undersize from regulation dimensions and show a placement that varied to say the least.

Some creative applications such as painting serial numbers aligned with the aircraft's ground angle rather than horizontal to the center axis can give the modeler a degree of leeway and a slightly different result. In contrast with reality, decals tend to provide the modeler with perfectly proportioned letters and numbers which sometimes need a degree of modification to make them match the real thing.

There are of course those who believe that they are totally unable to paint a straight line and

ABOVE Unpainted aircraft often featured different shades of metal on different panels. Individual panels were prepared by masking with Post-It Notes and Tamiya Masking Tape. Some panels were sprayed with Testor Metalizer Aluminum, while others received a coat of a darker shade.

BELOW The Olive Drab anti-glare panel on the front deck was masked and sprayed using Gunze acrylic Olive Drab. The natural metal finish was not over-sprayed with a flat finish after decals were added. A light coat of semi-gloss varnish was applied to the decals only.

RIGHT The P-47D's canopy was also painted silver. The clear sections of the framed canopy were masked with small strips of Tamiya masking tape. The first painting step was to spray black as a base coat.

RIGHT The canopy was then painted silver. Note that the insides of the clear parts have also been masked with tape. This is to avoid the risk of overspray on the inside.

RIGHT The result is a crisply painted set of canopy parts.

would be completely lost if they did not have access to decals, which is entirely understandable. As with any aspect of modeling, we all have a personal choice and preferences. For some subjects hand painting, or a mix and match combination of spraying and decals may yield more satisfactory results, depending on the subject.

PERSONAL MARKINGS

While not representing as large an artwork canvas for pin-ups, cartoons and names as the bombers, the tactical fighter outfits, particularly those attached to the 9th Air Force, had many P-47s, Mustangs and Lightnings covered with symbols representing combat missions. Along with names and cartoon figures, such aircraft had masses of bomb, broom, umbrella, train, truck, tank and ship symbols stenciled or painted on to record the destruction meted out to the enemy as the Allies swept across Europe.

Rows of small *Hakenkreuz*, *Balkenkreuz* or less commonly, the Regia Aeronautica's bundle of three fasces, recorded air and ground victories over German or Italian adversaries, some of them, it has to said, being more records of enthusiasm than actual kills. At the time, more than one pilot swore the enemy aircraft he fired at was a goner, a fact not always borne out by analysis of enemy records. Not that this matters in terms of model markings although a natural curiosity leads one to seek out the facts behind the symbols, the name of the pilot(s) and some of the sorties flown to accumulate the visible scoreboard.

The 9th Air Forces' cautious and even rather reluctant system of awarding aerial victories to its tactical pilots was the cause of some controversy, then and since. The curious "unconfirmed destroyed" was a category that frustrated numerous pilots and some seem to have painted the kill on their aircraft whatever higher authority's ruling was. This led to some P-47s particularly carrying impressive victory tallies, which do not bear out scrutiny of any list of aces. In this event *esprit de corps* was undoubtedly the main object of the exercise.

In the Pacific, similar embellishment of fighters took place, the rising sun or plainer "meatball" usually being used to indicate aerial victories. That said, there are numerous examples of variations on this basic theme, far more than any one modeler can ever duplicate over the average human lifetime!

Photos showing well decorated P-38s, P-40s, P-47s and P-51s might indicate the personal mount of an ace – or they may not. It is a well known fact that most of the top-scoring pilots used more than one aircraft to obtain their victories and in regard to tactical fighters, particularly those operating in Europe, there are for example numerous P-47s showing a row of kills which are not obviously attributed to any one pilot, but an accumulative score by several. Enough of these can be found in the pages of unit histories to start you on a research program to find out more. And there you have one more theme, several models of the different aircraft flown by one pilot.

Scores of USAAF fighters carried mission symbols in great profusion, making potentially excellent model subjects. Sometimes though, there is the problem of complete identification. Confronted with an interesting mission log, cartoon and name in a photograph showing only part of the aircraft, the modeler can have difficulty in unearthing details of the rest of the markings. This can lead to endless cross reference to all available books covering that particular type, but the search is often rewarded by the information required to complete a model. Some help is often provided.

The US practice of including the aircraft serial number on the forward fuselage data block has always been of great help (given a clear photographic reference) in identification of individual aircraft, even if only a partial front-end photo is available. The group and squadron code and serial number can usually be determined, leaving the confirmation of the individual aircraft code letter to be cracked. That can take more time. Some decal sheets miss out serial numbers for this very reason but the kit will be considered incomplete unless this detail can be unearthed.

However, more and more individual fighter markings are being perpetuated in fresh publications, magazine articles and ever more comprehensive decal sheets. There seems to be healthy competition among the various decal suppliers to come up with new schemes and their efforts should win nothing but praise from the modeler, as occasionally such data is not readily available elsewhere.

Decals have in fact become so accurate and sophisticated that they are turning themselves into an essential branch of research in their own right – to the point that the last thing anyone wants to do is cut them up for applying to a model!

It is at very least worthwhile running your eye over the lists of decals published regularly by mail order houses and modeling magazines to ensure that details of the aircraft you are looking for have not been added to any list. If it has, that may save you a considerable amount of time, should you have been intending to hand paint or cut up a selection of sheets to make up a complete serial number or set of code letters.

To my knowledge nobody has yet come up with faded and worn decals, irregular lines and markings stained with exhaust. If you want to make a model look totally authentic, all such irregularities, if relevant, should be included. Hand painting or the use of pre-shaped masks, can help obtain almost complete authenticity.

Final finishing using clear varnishes is perhaps an overlooked aspect of modeling but the popular ranges of paint include a variety of matt, gloss and sheen type finishes intended for spraying over the entire surface of the kit. Having relied on the semi-matt finish inherent in many modern paints, I've not had too much experience of what used to be simply termed varnishing. Otherwise I've found that a rub over with a soft cloth will bring up a sufficient sheen on a very matt surface – which leaves the ongoing problem of glossy decals contrasting a

BELOW Next we move to pre-shading weathering on an Olive Drab finish. Many World War 2 US Army Air Force fighters wore a finish of Olive Drab and Neutral Gray. Although even the names of the colors seem to imply an uninteresting paint job, Olive Drab actually resulted in a diverse finish due to its instability and heavy weathering in service. Pre-shading panel lines on a model offer the opportunity to lend even more definition to our Olive Drab P-39D Airacobra.

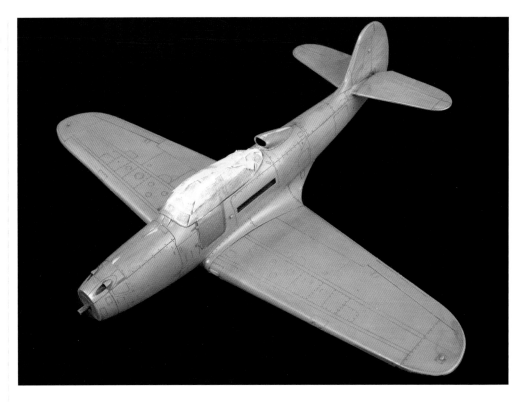

RIGHT The P-39D model was prepared by simply masking off the clear parts. The open "car door" on the starboard side was simply blanked off by taping the door in place.

little too much on the model paint surface. The vice versa challenge of very matt decals is not nearly so widespread. This decals-versus-paint contrast is where varnishes may come into their own but one should take into account the finish of the subject aircraft. Matt or semi-gloss black paintwork on aircraft such as the P-61 and P-38 often appears to show the national insignia glossier than surrounding airframe areas. This cannot always be the angle of the sun or the use of decals, but the effect is quite visible on photographs. It means that the application of a glossy commercial decal sheet to a matt finish will be authentic enough without the need to bring the model up to the sheen of the decals, which does seem to be a rather labor-intensive way to do things. As ever, the only answer is to give it a go on an old kit, principally to see how the varnish reacts with the decals and the softening agent, the thinners used in the paint and so forth.

MASKING

On a larger scale kit the simplest and most traditional form of mask is the hard demarcation line achieved by a card or stiff paper edge held lightly in position with tape, Blu Tack or even finger pressure. Carefully sprayed, the resultant lines on the kit should be crisp enough, with the advantage that the nose art, code letter, number or whatever, has exactly the same reflective property as the surrounding paint.

Any pliable material can be used to blank off pre-painted areas such as a cockpit interior and wheel wells, cotton wool or moistened tissue being particularly effective in eliminating any "creep " of sprayed paint.

Products such as Maskol are fine for some tasks although it has to be well mixed. Functioning by covering the masked off area with a fine, protective membrane, Maskol and other similar liquid products can shrink if the mix is not right. Stored for any length of time the product can harden and gel at the bottom of the container, in which case it is preferable to invest in a fresh supply. Older liquid mask may also have a tendency to "string" and not cover well.

Adhesive tape such as that sold expressly for the purpose by Tamiya may be used for masking small and large areas of models. The one proviso I'd add is to watch that a previously painted surface does not "lift" under the tape. Provided that it is lightly tacked down or used to anchor a piece of ordinary paper along the line to be painted, there should be few problems. I've found that silver (or aluminum shade) paint is prone to lifting as this has a tendency to "plate" the surface with slightly different adhesion properties to colors, depending on the type of paint being used. New tape with adhesion properties that may seem too strong can be wiped between thumb and forefinger before application to reduce its strength. Regular artwork masking tape or draughting tape is often recommended for this work but there is still the risk of getting too great an adhesion and even a hairy edge.

Masking tape's strength is achieved by a heavier material-like backing and should be used sparingly – it all depends on the complexity of the area to be masked – and whether in the case of the above-mentioned silver, if the model parts have been washed thoroughly before a start was made on construction. Constantly handling model parts can impart a coating that can be resistant to paint, so finger contact should be kept to a minimum.

If you prefer that the mask does not actually adhere to the surface of the model, it is possible to use tape to hold a paper or plastic edge down to do the actual "straight line" job by proximity spraying. The office stationery product Post-Its are ideal for this purpose as the adhesive line on the peel-off edge is gentle enough not to lift a paint surface.

There are now numerous custom peel off masks on the market, primarily for canopy frames and national insignia and many modelers will probably have used these or created their own similar methods, depending on what they are trying to achieve. It is well to remember that every eventuality for "creep" or overspray must be allowed for as paint will get through the smallest gaps unless great care is taken to prevent it doing so. But careful masking prior to application of paint for cowling nose rings and fuselage, wing and tail bands and so forth can sometimes be preferable to inducing decals to lay down on curved surfaces. Wheel hubs incidentally can be covered by circular self adhesive stickers that are sold in small sheets at stationery outlets. Available in a useful variety of sizes, they can protect the hub while the tire color is being sprayed.

CAMOUFLAGE MASKING

The biggest challenge some modelers of wartime fighters face is that of applying camouflage convincingly. The scale of the model does not really matter too much as the result should be similar. The question often posed in modeling journals is whether the paint shades should have hard or soft edges. And what is the preferred method of application – one overall color with the second one applied on top or the first coat applied over bare plastic with the second butting up across all surfaces? As regards edges and masking, one sees both applied – see the images accompanying this chapter for details of how to create both.

Both types of sprayed edge will be evident in reference photos and copying what is there will give good results: some areas, particularly those in shadow under the tailplane are impossible to check should a single monochrome photo be all that is available. In that instance all the modeler can do is to follow directives and paint charts that explain how paint patterns were generally applied to the type in question.

CANOPY FRAMES AND MASKING

Commercial companies have only recently appreciated that a market niche exists for carefully tailored, self-adhesive masks, but having identified it they are being offered in rapidly increasing numbers. Designed for use with specific aircraft types they are available

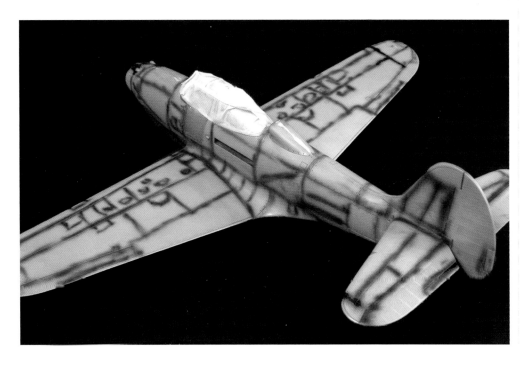

LEFT Panel lines on the P-39D were roughly over-sprayed using black acrylic paint. It is not necessary to be very precise at this stage.

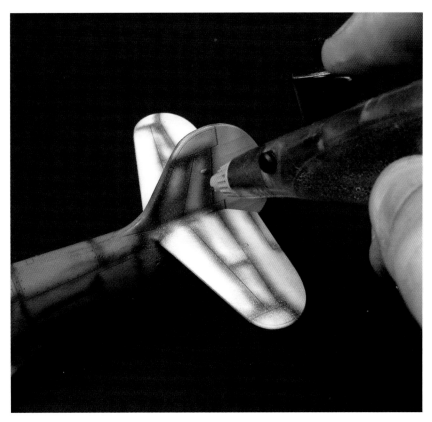

ABOVE Next, the top colors are next painted between the panel lines, resulting in a stark contrast. The top color was then over-sprayed in multiple light coats until the dark panel lines were barely visible. In the case of the P-39D, the white tail and leading edge markings were sprayed before the main camouflage colors.

this "instant canopy frame" method can be effective. It can certainly remove the hassle from what remains one of the most difficult tasks in model making. The one drawback is getting adhesive strips to adhere well. Over time they will have a tendency to dry out to the point of lifting off, so an adhesive suitable for such a job should be used, but very sparingly.

WHEELS

It is only comparatively recently that manufacturers have included treads on the tires of fighter kits, the bald variety having long been the norm. Fortunately there are kits that supply two sets of wheels, in flattened-under-load form and completely round. Such spares are valuable as treaded tires will considerably enhance an older kit. The patterns varied from type to type, so check your references.

Wheels are most easily painted when the hole in the hub is impaled on a round carrier such as a wooden or plastic cocktail stick. Suitably supported, bald tires can also be worked on to create convincing tread patterns in paint or small cuts, worn effects and "creep marks" which are often visible in very clear photos. Separate hubs might need some anchorage points for hydraulic lines and there is of course a need to paint the spokes of "open" wheels.

Hub cover plates over the wheel centers of American fighters commonly sported some form of decoration, in the form of stars, various designs in several colors or miniature insignia. In addition, more than a few added ID numbers for ground recognition on the flight line.

Should the kit decal sheet not run to these items the modeler may wish to add them, either by hand or after a delve through the spare decal file. Wheel cover plates – or the lack of them – is a sizeable subject on its own. Among the questions one can invariably ask is – were they always supplied with a given fighter type, irrespective of sub-type? If they were left off, was this usually because the presence of mud could accumulate dangerously and affect braking? Or were plates generally dropped on some sub-types later in the war, as photos would appear to indicate? I'm afraid I don't have the answers, either!

Kit wheels that traditionally were completely round until comparatively recently can be given flats by using a domestic iron. Heat the appliance just to the point where plastic will soften and place a suitable cushion between the surface and the model's wheels. I find that the

from companies such as Meteor Productions Inc. of Merrifield that has numerous subjects in the Black Magic range, while Eduard of the Czech Republic markets Express Mask.

These products serve to highlight one of the most demanding tasks in completing a model aircraft to a reasonably high standard. Ensuring that the windscreen and cockpit canopy framework is painted well can be the stuff of nightmares as there are few areas that will make or break an otherwise attractive finish. Not only does the shape of the cockpit framing have to be spot-on, all the lines have to be dead straight. Shaky lines are very quickly noticed, unfortunately. There are various ways around this problem if the hand holding a loaded brush insists on deviating from an extremely narrow frame line.

Pre-masking and spraying the canopy framework is a reliable method although much depends on how well defined these strips are (see the images on page 98.) Even slightly raised frame lines can be difficult as what you are actually doing is painting a strip with three sides. Rubbing the framework down is sometimes an option, proving that masking those panels that should be kept free of paint reduces the risk of scratching the clear areas. A further method is the application of strips of adhesive tape. Pre-painted, these strips may be cut very finely indeed; providing that the result does not have an over-scale appearance,

LEFT Eduard's P-39 kits include self-adhesive canopy masks. These greatly simplify the task of masking the canopy, but some care was required as the adhesive is not particularly strong. The edges of the masks were burnished with the end of a toothpick before spraying to avoid paint bleeding under the self-adhesive material. The white tail and wing leading edges were also masked at this stage.

tissue provided as kit decal protection is ideal for this purpose. Stand the model on the iron's surface, making sure that it is level. Gentle pressure will soon flatten the bottom of the tires. With a large kit that won't three-point on the iron, the appliance will have to be held level with a table or other surface to ensure that the tail or nosewheel is flattened in equal degrees. Equally, the wheels can be flattened separately but if they're not attached to their oleos there is the risk that the flats will be uneven.

In regard to wheels and tires, it is well worth the time to check that what comes in the kit bears a close resemblance to the real thing. Historically kit wheels were often too thin in cross section and some fighters, notably the P-40, had wheels that appear almost disproportionately large. Some digging in the spares box will be necessary to come up with the right size if you feel that the kit wheels need to be changed.

GUNS

As one of the major components in plastic kits of military aircraft, replica guns require special treatment. They should of course not look the same as tires or propeller blades, the other two "black" areas of wartime airplanes. Kit paint instructions would have you believe otherwise, offering as they do little in the way of guidance.

A coat of matt blue/black is indeed necessary but only as a starting point.

Many kit machine guns are molded convincingly with enough engraved detail and require only a "metallic" look to enhance their authenticity. Paints formulated to have a metallic look are useful but don't overlook another method of imparting this effect to paintwork which is about as simple as it gets.

Graphite from the humble pencil, rubbed on with a finger or tissue, is a remarkably effective weathering device. Pencils are a surprisingly useful and perhaps overlooked model aid. Shaved off lead (any soft grade from HB to 6B can be used) is simply applied to black-painted guns to impart a realistic gunmetal sheen to the surface of the barrel jacket and breech block. It is also easy to pencil directly onto the surface of the plastic to add depth to the sheen.

The graphite method can also be used to enhance dark engine parts, particularly radial cylinders and to an extent on silver surfaces to create a dark weathering effect. As graphite is very smooth, a touch of it added to a plastic propeller boss will enable the blades to turn more easily. I also use a pencil to pick out areas of wheel wells that have engraved hydraulic and electrical lines. At the opposite end of the weathering spectrum, white chalk can be employed to lighten dark paint surfaces.

ABOVE The camouflage colors, Olive Drab and Neutral Gray, were sourced from the Polly Scale acrylic range. These colors were applied using the same technique as the white – first filling in between the panel lines, then successive lightly over-sprayed coats until the desired effect is achieved. The pre-shading can be seen under the Olive Drab, but it is not too obvious: subtlety is the objective.

MIRRORS

Rear-view mirrors are among the areas where fighter models might be improved. Most types had them to a greater or lesser degree, but they were particularly popular on Mustangs. I once noted that 8th Air Force P-51 B/C and D models had at least 25 different mirror mountings, both on the windscreen framework and the sliding canopy.

Many of the mirrors seen on USAAF aircraft in England were originally manufactured for Spitfires and Hurricanes and their mountings varied from a self-supporting single stem and the less common type with a second additional brace angled to impart strength. It appears that most rear-view mirrors fitted to US fighters in Europe continued to come from local sources, but there were American factory produced mirrors. On some batches of P-51Ds they were set into an additional small bubble in the main, sliding part of the canopy. Many Mustang kits now include mirrors but you may wish to add a second, which was quite a common practice, should you opt to finish a model depicting the markings of a particular pilot. Usually the choice of mirror was personal to the man flying the aircraft, as it was he alone who needed the extra vision behind him in combat. Once more, the references need checking closely to see what style was fitted to the aircraft you are modeling.

BASEBOARDS & DISPLAYS

The widespread adoption of baseboards for individual models enables interesting information about the subject to be presented "at a glance." Depending on what needs to be included here, the modeler can give his imagination a free rein by rendering the badge of the parent unit the model in question belonged to, adding a photo of the full-size aircraft and perhaps, brief written data on the pilot(s) who flew it in combat. For competition entries, some people prefer to provide notes on the model and mention any conversion work they have carried out, although such data can be presented on a separate card if the organizers prefer it.

RIGHT Individual panels on the P-39D were outlined with Tamiya masking tape in preparation for the application of alternate shades of Olive Drab. The base color was lightened with a few drops of Polly Scale US Desert Sand. The fabric-coated ailerons received an even paler shade of Olive Drab, as these surfaces faded dramatically in service.

A base can, alternatively, be just that if you interpret the word as a fighter dispersal area. Much depends on the scale of the kit standing on it and what else you intend to display. Three-dimensional items such as oil drums are minimalist accessories but if the base area is larger, a fuel bowser or other vehicles may be included. Placing the aircraft itself on pierced steel planking is always effective and a number of manufacturers have in the past offered flexible sheets of PSP in various scales that need to be attached to a firm base board. One I've used was an American product called Scalegrate which, as it incorporates a few tears and indication of repair, makes a very authentic front-line baseboard.

Eduard market bases in rigid plastic with the PSP effect forming the surface upon which the model stands. Originally available in 265mm by 164mm size, suitable for a single-engine fighter up to 1/48 scale, the range has since been extended to include bases double that size. Very widely used on the often rough front-line airfields employed by USAAF fighter groups, this handy, instant runway material sets off a well-made model arguably better than any other if a realistic, as opposed to an artistic, setting is required.

As should be obvious from the above, a clear division exists between a realistic and a designed base, both of which are a step up from plain ones. The latter may well be the modeler's choice for the quite understandable reason that, having slaved over the model, the urge to put the same dedication into a base is not nearly so strong! Fortunately, plain bases, particularly those carved from fine-grained wood, look attractive enough and to some eyes, do not detract in any way from the model itself. That's also a valid point and one that the modeler who wishes his work not to be judged as a diorama will have to consider if he is building for competition display. The problem is that modern model competitions feature so many bases that models placed directly onto the display table are starting to look as though they have something missing

There are numerous alternative types of baseboard that need not be very time consuming to create. Simply cutting up and pasting down a well rendered piece of box art and/or the kit instruction sheet on stiff card to your own design can work well. Almost any rigid surface that will support a model can suffice, including mirror tiles which can be butted together to form as large an area as necessary to show off any additional detail added to the model's lower surfaces. This also safeguards against anyone picking the model up to check if the undersides have been finished correctly and possibly causing damage.

AIRFIELD VEHICLES

Fuel bowsers have already been touched upon but the range of airfield vehicles as injection-molded kit suitable for display with AAF fighter models is not exactly vast. In 1/72 scale the Hasegawa Mini Box range of tanks and military vehicles included a six-wheel GMC CCKW-353 Gasoline Tank Truck, complete with a 57th Fighter Group P-47 on the box top. This kit, which ran to a two-man crew but not a flexible fuel hose, was nicely detailed for the scale although such items as wire mesh guards

on lights always need replacing on military vehicle kits, irrespective of the scale.

Several other items in the Hasegawa range, including a Wilys Jeep, a smaller size bowser and two different trucks, were all intended for or could be adapted to, aircraft dioramas. As is well known, the build-up of the 8th Air Force in Britain was given much *matériel* support by the British before US equipment was shipped over the Atlantic. Therefore model items such as the Airfix RAF Recovery Set, consisting of a Bedford OX tractor unit for a Queen Mary trailer and a Coles Mk 7 crane on a Thornycroft Amazon chassis, can also be adapted for an American airfield scene. The same applies to the Airfix RAF Emergency Set. This comprised a pair of vehicles, the K.2 ambulance and the K.6 crash tender, both on Austin chassis.

In regard to figures, Airfix put out several 1/72 (HO/OO) scale aircrew sets including "USAAF Personnel" which offered "46 pieces making 38 assemblies," to quote the box top. The extra pieces consisted of a single 500 lb bomb and a one-man jack trolley. An excellent photo of this device in use at a P-47 base appears on page 111 of Roger Freeman's book *The Fight for the Skies* published by Arms and Amour Press.

I have not come across a great many airfield vehicles since the above kits were first released in the 1970s but must also admit to not looking out for new additions to any great extent either, so I may be a little out of date as to what is currently available. I do know that some extra work is necessary if the modeler wishes to attach the fuel

ABOVE and RIGHT Additional weathering included highlighting of panel lines with a thin wash of black oil paint applied directly to the recessed lines. Finally, exhaust stains and oil streaks were added using a thin mix of Tamiya Flat Black and Red Brown. The dramatic pattern of streaks and stains on the lower fuselage was carefully copied from a photograph of a wartime P-39D on page 17 of Bert Kinzey's *P-39 Airacobra In Detail*.

lines from the bowser to the aircraft and that such a scene almost certainly demands the inclusion of a figure or two, as ground crew were hardly in the habit of departing for a smoke and leaving a few hundred gallons of high octane gasoline to pump into the wing and/or fuselage tanks on their own!

In 1/48 scale the airfield support vehicle picture has not been quite so rosy as manufacturers long ago adopted 1/35 as the standard scale for the larger military vehicle kit. While certain items in this scale are adaptable to aircraft in 1/32 scale, vehicles suitable for display with 1/48-scale aircraft have been somewhat neglected, as least as far as the mainstream manufacturers are concerned. In partial response to this dearth, Monogram included a Cletrac tractor in their B-24 Liberator kit and this, despite a molding that was a little "chunky" and detail that was on the basic side, was a very welcome extra. For a baseboard display a fighter can be hooked up to the Cletrac via tow bars fixed to the landing gear oleos – once again, do check the references to see exactly where these fitted on different aircraft types. As it comes, the Cletrac has "solid" sidewalls between the tracks, lacks windscreen glass and any hint that the vehicle was equipped with a soft-top canvas hood – a vital extra for English and Italian winters. All these details and others, can be added without difficulty to the Monogram kit although references will also indicate that Cletracs operated with the windscreen folded flat.

As a companion to the B-24 tractor, the Monogram B-17G included a flatbed bomb trailer. No motive power was actually provided in

the kit but this trailer was commonly hooked up to a Cletrac or a truck for moving out to the flight line. Most commonly photographed on bomber bases, these important vehicles are equally adaptable to a fighter scene where they carried oxygen bottles as well as bombs, rockets and ammunition boxes.

References to vehicles directly associated with the operation of USAAF fighters are not, to my knowledge, too thick on the ground although all encompassing references such as the *Mighty Eighth War Manual* does include some basic details and no less than 17 photographs in the chapter entitled Ground Support Equipment. Obviously majoring on

ABOVE Now we come to creating post-shaded weathering for a Desert Warhawk, as shown here on the P-40F.

BELOW AMtech's 1/48-scale P-40F was painted with Polly Scale acrylic paints – Azure Blue on the lower surfaces and a base coat of RAF Middle Stone on the fuselage sides and the top of the model. A few minor gaps were dealt with using Gunze Mr Surfacer before painting continued – it is never too late to find (and fix) a problem.

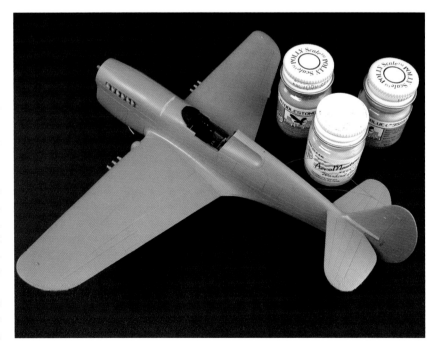

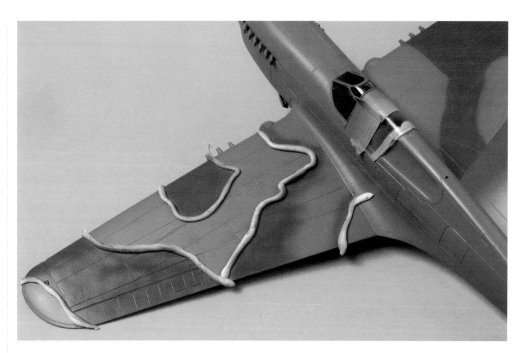

RIGHT The disruptive camouflage on desert P-40s had a hard edge. In order to replicate this edge, Blu-Tack was rolled into thin sausages and gently applied to the surface in the shape of the camouflage pattern. Polly Scale Dark Earth was then sprayed inside the Blu-Tack border, resulting in a hard edge with the tiniest hint of narrow overspray.

materiel supplied to the 8th Air Force in the UK from both British and American sources, this reference extends to ambulances, wreckers, mobile cranes and runway control vehicles and trailers, the latter decked out with a distinctive black and white checkerboard finish for high visibility out on airfields.

Some general guides to military vehicles of World War 2 such as the *Observer's Fighting Vehicles Directory* published by Warne, include airfield equipment. My aging edition has proved quite useful in this respect and although more modern titles appertaining to the subject have no doubt appeared recently. Numerous vehicles will be observed within the pages of general fighter group histories; so with a diorama in mind, now is the time to go over them again and take a second look at the vehicles you may have missed the first time around.

As a last word on this aspect of aircraft modeling it is not wise to assume that fighter units in other theaters of war were supplied with vehicles and so on to the extent that the European-based air forces were. In the CBI, for example, a beat-up Chinese truck or an ox cart might be more appropriate than a custom-built trailer for carrying bombs, the units based there being situated at the end of very long supply lines.

THEMES

With the aim of branching out into aircraft color schemes that are that little bit different, individual modelers often pool their work into a group project with a common theme. The IPMS Special Interest Groups – SIGs – have spurred this approach to modeling and the results of combining the resources of small or large groups of modelers can be seen to advantage at numerous shows. The internet has undoubtedly assisted this coming together of the SIGs.

In fact many themes suggest themselves to models of American fighters. They might include aircraft flown by the aces, different aircraft used by the same squadron or group, depicting the ever-popular black and white stripes applied for D-Day in Europe or the invasion of the Philippines and the famous sharkmouth marking, carried at various times in different war theaters, by all first-line US fighter types.

Simple, common themes might include the use of stripes and/or checkers as unit markings; the ever popular ladies in various stages of undress; aircraft decorated with the names of the cartoon characters made famous by Al Capp, Walt Disney and others – even aircraft with the same nickname might appeal to some groups of modelers.

Characters from comic strips, movie and song titles provided the wartime US serviceman with a wide range of inspiration when it came to naming combat aircraft. Not all names are readily traceable to their source however and a working knowledge of American sports and card games in vogue during the war can help to crack some of the expressions used to personalize aircraft in this way.

One variation on the theme idea is to set out specifically to duplicate in plastic an individual aircraft in a photos or photos. "Mrs Virginia" a

LEFT The arial wires were attached to the model prior to painting, eliminating the risk of spoiling the paint job with smudges of superglue. Patches of Olive Drab were also added on the assumption that the RAF fin flash and starboard side wing markings would have been painted out. Later advice suggested that these aircraft probably never carried the RAF wing markings, so the Olive Drab circle was lightly sanded and repainted with the camouflage colors.

P-51A of the 1st Air Commando Group is well enough known and an ideal choice. With engine exhaust stretching over half the length of the fuselage, this example offers one of the best weathering subjects anywhere.

Along similar themed lines are aircraft painted up specially to mark a milestone such as the 15,000th P-40N with all the customer national insignia. Enough "round the clock" halftone and color photos have been published for such a model to be completed with satisfying accuracy, using the Create 301 kit. Modeling commemorative aircraft need not stop there as dozens of P-47s sported similar markings to record milestones in production and those denoting their purchase through war bond drives. Most well known of all in this category perhaps is the P-38J painted in overall bright red with the wording "Yippee" under the wings. The difference here of course is that the Thunderbolts saw action while the others did not.

Themes can naturally extend to an attractive display base for the finished model. A plain sheet of clear plastic will protect photographs of the full-size aircraft, a portrait of the famous pilot(s) who flew it, artwork profiles of aircraft of the same unit, or an original unit badge in the form of a cloth patch or a decal; these are just some ideas.

BUILD A BONEYARD

Throughout the foregoing text there has at least been the implication that after a few years at the hobby a modeler will have acquired a goodly range of spare parts. This might come about in a number of ways not least via the younger generation. To be brutally realistic about plastic modeling, it is often only a passing phase of growing up; youngsters will just as soon throw a kit together for the sole purpose of blowing it to bits on Guy Fawkes night or speed its partial demise in some other dire way. Such a fate may be anathema to the more mature modeler but he or she can benefit from this vandalism by collecting the left over bits and removing them to a safe place on the grounds of clearing up. Few parents will complain once the wrecker of kits has discovered a range of alternative interests, from computer games to – well, you name it!

The hoarding modeler with a few young relatives can therefore soon be inundated with a mass – even a mess – of truncated wings and fuselages, wheels, props and what have you. Some parts indeed come in handy for conversion work but most of the larger items tend to languish in the spares box inevitably to be joined by the leftovers from the modeler's own kit bashing efforts. As the years pass, the three P-51s, four P-40s and two P-38s (any combination of numbers is applicable to some of us) which were once the latest thing but which you never got around to completing, are rendered more or less obsolete by newer, more accurate kits. Deep down, you know you'll never build these older ones now. Do they have any use?

If the major components have been separated from the sprues, or you have boxes full of previously painted kits now broken down for easy storage (on the grounds that one day they might be used again), they certainly do.

RIGHT Post-shading commenced with a thin wash of black oil paint precisely applied to the recessed panel lines.

One method is to stack all the wings and fuselages together on a baseboard, put all the wheels in a separate heap, along with the spinners, cockpit canopies, drop tanks and so on, and you have an instant corner of a scrap yard in the making. Take a baseboard in the size required, run a section of fence in any material preferred from card to metal around two sides of it and simply arrange the model parts on the base and against the fence. Chances are some of the wings and fuselages will have old paint and decals still in place – so much the better, as they will provide a touch of variety. It goes without saying that models to any scale may be used for a boneyard scene although surplus 1/72-scale kits must be the most economical – and probably the most numerous.

It is perfectly possible, of course, to super detail such a diorama in much the same way as any other; but the beauty of the basic scrap heap is that with some judicious placement, you can get away with the minimum of gluing and painting. It does help if you have a number of examples of the one aircraft type as, tidy to the end, the military tended, at least in the US, to park similar aircraft types together while they awaited their fate. Poor surface detail or any outline inaccuracies of the parts can be all but be hidden by carefully composing the scene; wings stacked on their edge do not reveal much and neither do fuselages if they are tightly packed together in a line. Paint may be dabbed on the leading or trailing edges of the wings that are most visible to enhance the

effect and where appropriate, the US national insignia may be overpainted and depicted as a solid shape. Color photos show the shade used to have been rust red in one instance but there were others.

If you do tackle such a project, don't overlook that box of old, brittle decals that are not likely be applied to any current model. Cut them up and apply where appropriate to those areas of the scrap wings and fuselages that may be seen.

The modeler can tailor such a display to taste. A P-40 for example, placed in front of the stacked airframe parts on its gear legs with its windscreen in place, will set the scene well enough and provide a focus. Alternatively, the Pacific island "hole in the ground" type of scrap scene, with P-38s and P-61s (some with drop tanks still attached) shoved on top of truncated bomber parts, might be a more ambitious project for some people. The references are full of these sad but necessary scenes of 1945 as the Allies systematically scrapped the largest air forces the world had ever seen.

Aircraft disposal came into three broad categories: firstly, those where the scrapping of surplus but complete airframes took place, mainly in the US; secondly there were the locations where aircraft were stripped of military equipment and put up for sale; and thirdly were those areas – mainly overseas – where combat damaged aircraft carcasses were simply abandoned. A sub-category might be the "active" wartime scrap yard from which

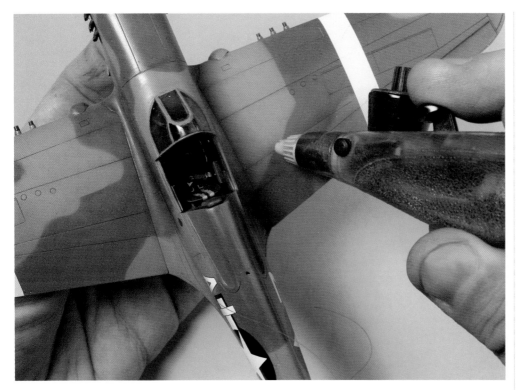

LEFT Once this step was complete, a very thin mix of Flat Black and Red Brown was sprayed over the panel lines. In common with the pre-shading technique, a subtle finish is the objective.

airframes were cannibalized for spares to keep other aircraft flying.

In modeling terms, each type of dump requires a different approach. For the open air "hangar queen," some deliberate stripping might be desirable, not to mention a degree of airframe damage from shot and shell, a wheels–up landing and so forth. Missing panels, bent propeller blades and some cutting away of the airframe to reveal the structure underneath,

are all areas the skilled modeler can tackle to make such a scene that much more realistic. This is where those saved pieces of flash can come in handy as the thin plastic makes ideal damaged panels.

Finally, the references contain numerous scenes of aircraft being readied for the smelter. In the US these machines were stripped of engines, tires, props and so forth and were stacked prior to disposal in a much more organized manner.

LEFT Kit decals were added at this stage.

American master modeler Shepherd Paine is a master of this sort of presentation, and has based many of his creations on Monogram kits. An abandoned and vandalized B-25 Mitchell came as part of the package in the original 1/48-scale kit. There was also a ditching scene with the TBD Devastator kit – these and a whole range of other ideas are readily adaptable to fighters. Shep published a book, *How to Build Dioramas* in 1980, an A4 format paperback crammed with ideas including an amazing B-26 Marauder production line. Such an ambitious and innovative modeling project will appeal to many, with the advantage of some space saving if adapted to reproducing part of a factory turning out single-engine fighters.

A further variation on this theme is an arming area. By placing a P-47 next to a stack of bombs and M-10 rocket launchers you can also reduce your stocks of plastic ordnance, which proliferates with every kit you buy these days. A last thought – if you are a voracious modeler who uses many spares, leave the boneyard scenes intact on the shelf, so at least you can see at a glance how many props, wheels or canopies you actually have without the need to sort through ten different storage boxes!

WHERE TO STORE THEM?

Finally, there is the ever present problem of storing models once they have been completed, and unless you live in a converted Zeppelin shed you'll soon find that space is at a premium. Dust very quickly settles on the surface of a plastic model which itself just sits there, eating into an area that you really need for yet another reference book – or indeed another model.

I can't suggest a ready answer apart from the none-too-satisfactory remedy of hanging models from the ceiling. Up there they will gather dust faster than almost anywhere else and short of repacking them into boxes, with some risk of breaking off the smaller more delicate parts, this remains a challenge proportionate to the amount of available space. Friends of mine have wisely built display cabinets that are intended to line walls or alcoves.

If the only option is to pack completed models away, a visit to your local wine merchant might yield a number of wooden boxes. These come complete with supporting inserts to hold the neck of the bottles firmly. A box intended for a couple of bottles will actually hold a 1/48-scale P-47 or P-51 nicely with room to spare for additional cushioning material such as bubble-wrap. A further model storage idea is a box with a transparent lid. Large enough to house a 1/32 scale P-51 with its wheels down, these boxes are a bit flimsy and it is advisable to remove the propeller. But a well-fitting see-through top of this type does keep out the dust and prevents the model from being completely hidden from view. A sort of bonus here is that if the model is unfinished but visible you can always nag yourself into completing it some day soon.

I have in the past built a floor-to-ceiling stacking unit so that you have a number of

LEFT A final coat of Polly Scale acrylic/flat finished off this project.

shelves available. Measured on the size of the baseboard for the largest kit you have, these will then serve as a useful resting place for smaller kits, and a number of completed models and/or boxes can be accommodated. Many stores now sell modular shelf units designed to squeeze into the smallest possible space, and these are well worth investigating to meet your personal requirements. Most practical of all are glass-fronted cabinets, cupboards or model display cases which allow the models to be seen and which inhibit the ingress of the dreaded dust.

If your living room runs to a large coffee table this might be adapted to take an enclosed shelf unit for models, viewed through a glass top.

It is however a sad fact that many of the models made up do eventually fall into disrepair through lack of safe storage space and although all the pieces that come adrift are dutifully kept, there is some inbuilt resistance to refurbishing if the choice is between taking the time to do the necessary remedial work all over again, or tackling a new kit.

Garden shed or garage storage of models is another possibility but in these locations, absolute freedom from damp cannot always be guaranteed, with a consequent detrimental effect on the decals and maybe even the paint finish. Overtime some decals will yellow, crack and peel off – apart that is from those you may want to remove to refurbish a kit that may no longer be available.

If you do have to resign yourself to storage which risks breakage, it is a good idea to photograph each model as you complete it. That way even if it plunges to the floor the next time you attempt to find something in the stack of boxes underneath it, at least you will have a record of the way it used to look.

A last resort alternative to your own storage is to present built up models to a local history or war museum, if one exists with space available. There are numerous small establishments such as control tower museums adjacent to historic airfields. Often run on a shoestring, such locations may be glad of some additional display items, especially if your model subjects are relevant to the units that were once based on the airfield in question. It may only take a phone call or an e-mail to check.

Table 2: USAAF ordnance colors

Bombs (various weights and types including HE general purpose, light case, TNT or Amatol filled; armor-piercing and semi-armor piercing and fragmentation)	matt olive drab body 1in. yellow nose ring(s) with black stencil-style wording on body 1in. yellow after-body single ring (or two to denote RDX filling) just forward of fins; special filling denoted by black wording on one nose and one tail band for maximum readability
GP or LC, Tritonal filled	0.5in. yellow band between two 1in. bands on nose and tail. NMF tail fuse gear and locking nut on extreme nose, usually contrasted by yellow spot on extreme forward flat area common to all bombs.
120 lb M-41 fragmentation bomb	yellow nose rings; olive drab body and fins; black stencil-style wording
Photoflash bombs	gray, no bands; black markings
4.5in. M-10 rocket launcher tubes	dark green/olive drab exterior with red interior
M-8 projectile	olive drab body; yellow head
4.5in. HVAR	olive drab head; steel body and fins
4.5in. HVAR	half yellow/half NMF head and body on shaped charge type; steel body and fins
4.5in. HVAR	red nose, white body, red fins (practice round)

Table 3: Drop-tank colors

Early metal (teardrop-shaped) 75 gal. drop tanks painted to match underside color of aircraft	usually neutral gray or light gray; some in olive drab
Impregnated paper tanks (108 gal. capacity)	NMF (silver doped) with two red bands on center section
Metal (steel) tanks (108 gal.)	light gray with two red bands; some in dark olive drab
Elongated teardrop (150–165 gal.) commonly carried by P-38 and P-47N	NMF or painted to match aircraft finish, particularly black on night fighters
All tank filler caps	red

THE GALLERY

LEFT Lockheed P-38 Lightning, model by Chris Wauchop. This is Hasegawa's 1/48-scale P-38J Lightning kit. The panel lines and surface detail are well rendered on this model. It also portrays the graceful lines of this twin-boomed fighter beautifully. However, the kit is best suited to experienced modelers due to the alignment challenges presented by the architecture of the aircraft, and the relatively complex kit engineering presented by Hasegawa.

LEFT The P-38 was originally built by another modeler and reconditioned by Chris. He left the existing decals in place and actually airbrushed around them. The model was repainted using Gunze acrylic paints in a Testor Aztek airbrush.

LEFT This model features impressive weathering of its Olive Drab and Neutral Gray finish. Panel lines have been over-sprayed with a thin mix of black and brown, then the recessed lines have been further highlighted with a thin acrylic wash. Paint damage and chips were created using Tamiya Silver enamel paint applied with a fine brush.

RIGHT This overhead view highlights the patchy finish, which is typical of wartime Olive Drab paint on USAAF fighters in the Pacific and in Europe. The top canopy section was replaced with the equivalent section from a Falcon vacuform canopy set. A pilot was also added to the interior of the model. Nylon monofilament (invisible mending thread) was used for the aerial wire.

RIGHT The exhaust from the supercharger is a chalky gray/tan color. Tamiya Buff, a little White and some Flat Base were mixed to achieve this convincing effect. Paint damage on the wing walkway beside the cockpit can also be seen in this view.

TOP Curtiss P-40E, model by Brett Green. This is AMtech's 1/48-scale P-40 Warhawk. The cockpit in the kit is a little bare so a True Details resin cockpit was added. This set was actually designed for the Mauve P-40N, but it was eventually persuaded to fit in the AMtech fuselage with a little help from a razor saw and sanding stick.

MIDDLE The side view shows off the distinctive deep chin intake, the additional intake on top of the cowling, the framed canopy and the original short tail.

BOTTOM The model was finished with one of AMtech's high quality decal options supplied with the kit. The paint finish is fascinating. The basic camouflage colors are Dark Earth and Dark Green, but large patches have been over-painted in a darker color – possibly fresh Olive Drab. The shark's mouth and the irreverent character on the tail lend even more interest to this subject. The disruptive color scheme was painted with the assistance of Black Magic self-adhesive camouflage masks. The set I used was actually intended for a P-40B Tomahawk but the pattern was similar and it was a simple matter to adapt the masks to the different contours of this later version. A combination of Gunze and Polly Scale paints were used. The Olive Drab patches were sprayed freehand. The kit canopy rides high on the fuselage spine when depicted open, so a vacuform replacement was sourced from Squadron. The ring and bead sight came from an Eduard photo-etched set (not for a P-40 though), a mirror on top of the windscreen was carved from a scrap of styrene block and the twin antenna wires were added from smoke-colored invisible mending thread.

RIGHT P-40N Warhawk, model by Darren Mottram. Mauve from Japan released three 1/48-scale P-40 kits in the mid-1990s. This P-40N Warhawk is the first of these offerings. The model features excellent surface details with crisply engraved panel lines. Clear parts are very thin and free of distortion, but the fit of the clear section behind the cockpit can cause some alignment headaches.

RIGHT The True Details resin cockpit was added to this kit. True Details' cockpit is inexpensive and quite nicely detailed – an excellent replacement for the basic kit cockpit. True Details resin wheels were also used.

RIGHT Mauve's P-40 was painted with AeroMaster enamels. Although the same markings are included in the kit, SuperScale decals were employed for this project. In fact, two sets of the parrot's head were applied to guarantee complete opacity of the bright colors.

LEFT Republic P-47D Thunderbolt, model by Darren Mottram. Academy's 1/48-scale P-47D kit was released around the same time as Hasegawa's offering. Apart from some questions about the shape of the canopy it is a very nice kit with a straightforward fit. The shape of the model is accurate too.

LEFT Construction presented no problems and the model was completed almost without modification. The only addition was an extra rib added inside each side of the wheelwell to cover a kit join-line. The kit cockpit was also used straight from the box.

LEFT Some British-based P-47s used stocks of RAF paints to camouflage their aircraft. Although it is at odds with the instructions, the box art depicts a Thunderbolt finished in RAF Dark Green and RAF Sky with a Neutral Gray fuel tank. The box art served as the inspiration for the paint job. Xtracolour enamels were used for the RAF colors. Weathering comprised Tamiya Smoke being sprayed along the panel lines for subtle highlighting. Kit decals were used for the most part. The exception was the impressively checkered nose. This was masked with individual squares of Tamiya masking tape and sprayed!

RIGHT Republic P-47N Thunderbolt, model by Mick Evans. Academy's 1/48-scale P-47N Thunderbolt represents the final production version of this bulky USAAF fighter aircraft. Academy's kit was released around the same time as the ProModeler kit. The Academy kit features superior surface detail and less troublesome fit than its ProModeler counterpart.

RIGHT Academy's 1/48-scale P-47N supplies a generous allowance of stores including bombs, rockets and drop tanks. Much of this ordnance can be seen fitted to the model.

RIGHT The model was built straight from the box. The natural metal finish was achieved using Testor's Metalizer Buffable Aluminum. Alternate shades were also obtained on randomly selected panels by mixing different Metalizer shades. Decals were sourced from AeroMaster.

LEFT North American P-51A Mustang, model by Darren Mottram. The mid-1990s saw a flood of 1/48-scale P-51 Mustangs hit the market. ProModeler, Tamiya and Accurate Miniatures all released P-51B/C kits within 12 months of each other. However, Accurate Miniatures maintained an exclusive hold on the 1/48-scale Allison-powered Mustang variants. Accurate Miniatures released a P-51, P-51A, A-36 and an RAF Mustang Mk. I in 1/48 scale.

LEFT This is Accurate Miniatures' 1/48-scale P-51A kit, built straight from the box except for the canopy, which was sliced apart to fix in the open position. This extraordinary camouflage was referred to as the "dazzle scheme," and also sometimes as "confusion camouflage." It was painted as an experimental measure in the United States during 1943. The Olive Drab paint was from the Xtracolour range. Black and white paints were Humbrol enamels.

LEFT To obtain this striking finish, the model was first sprayed white all over. The fuselage and lower wings were then completely covered with Tamiya masking tape. The dazzle pattern was drawn onto the masking tape using a wartime photograph as reference. A sharp knife was then employed to trace over the pencil lines and cut out the black sections of the camouflage. Humbrol Flat Black was then sprayed, followed by more masking and painting of the Olive Drab upper surfaces. Markings were minimal – one upper wing roundel and a few stencils.

TOP LEFT North American P-51B Mustang, by Chris Wauchop. Tamiya's 1/48-scale P-51B Mustang was released in 1995, and was an immediate hit with modelers. The kit includes drop tanks, bombs, and alternative exhausts.

TOP RIGHT The P-51B was painted with Gunze acrylic paints in a Testor Aztek A470 airbrush. Weathering comprised the shading of panel lines, stains on panels and chipping of wing leading edges and fasteners. "Chipping" the paint was achieved using a sharp silver pencil. AeroMaster decals were used on this model.

BOTTOM LEFT This Mustang was built straight from the box except for the drop tanks. The open canopy is supplied as an optional assembly, with the open top molded to the starboard side of the canopy. The fit of the flaps was so good that glue was not required.

BOTTOM RIGHT The only addition to the kit cockpit was the pilot's harness, scratchbuilt from lead foil for the straps and fine wire for the buckles. This photo offers a fine view of Chris's wonderful weathering on the wing walk and fasteners.

APPENDICES

APPENDIX A – USEFUL ADDRESSES AND WEBSITES

American Air Museum
c/o Imperial War Museum
Duxford
CAMBS CB2 4QR
UK
The American Air Museum in Britain acts as a memorial to the 30,000 Americans who died flying from the UK in World War 2, and houses a collection of historic American combat aircraft.

American Aviation Historical Society
2333 Otis Street
Santa Ana
CA 92704-3846
USA
Excellent quarterly journal devoted to all aspects of US aviation history.

The Aviation Bookshop
656 Holloway Road
London N19 3PD
UK
Long-established book supplier carrying a full range of literature including books, modeling periodicals, plans and photographs.

Aviation Usk
602 Front St
Box 97
Usk WA 99180
USA
Model mail-order house and publisher specializing in rare kits and publications worldwide.

Hannants
Harbour Road
Oulton Broad
Lowestoft
Suffolk NR32 3LZ
UK
Internationally renowned mail-order suppliers specializing in kits and accessories from around the world.

Imperial War Museum
Department of Photographs
All Saint's Annexe
Austral St
London SE11 6SJ
UK
With a collection of several million prints and negatives, the IWM can supply numerous good quality aircraft images.

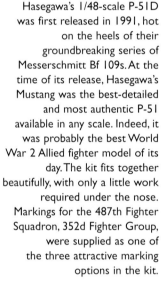

BELOW North American P-51D Mustang, model by Mick Evans. Hasegawa's 1/48-scale P-51D was first released in 1991, hot on the heels of their groundbreaking series of Messerschmitt Bf 109s. At the time of its release, Hasegawa's Mustang was the best-detailed and most authentic P-51 available in any scale. Indeed, it was probably the best World War 2 Allied fighter model of its day. The kit fits together beautifully, with only a little work required under the nose. Markings for the 487th Fighter Squadron, 352d Fighter Group, were supplied as one of the three attractive marking options in the kit.

**International Plastic Modelers Society –
USA**
Membership Secretary
c/o IPMS/USA
PO Box 2475
North Canton
OH 4720-2475
USA
Annual membership includes a quarterly maga-
zine carrying articles, news, reviews and web sites.

Just Bases
Mr P Thompson
21 Graham Road
Paignton
Devon TQ3 1BB
UK
As the name implies, this firm makes and
supplies finished bases and covered display
cases including the glass-dome type for
protection from dust.

Koster Aero Enterprises
25 Glenridge Drive
Bedford
MA 01730
USA
Suppliers of high quality vacuform and
multi-media kits

Paragon Designs
39 Cantley Lane
Norwich
Norfolk NR4 6TA
UK
Extensive range of resin "extras" for numerous
kits in various scales.

US Air Force Museum
1100 Spaatz St.
Wright-Patterson AFB
OH 45433
USA
The USAF Museum is located near Dayton,
Ohio, and is the oldest and largest military
aviation museum in the world. Its exhibits
include over 300 aircraft and missiles.

Verlinden Productions
811 Lone Star Drive   *(UK Distributors:*
O'Fallon   *Historex Agents*
MO 63366   *Wellington House*
USA   *157 Snargate Street*
                          Dover, Kent, UK)
Verlinden's well established range of kit
conversion sets and accessories includes many
USAAF subjects: it also publishes a
complementary series of modeling books.

WEBSITES
Hyperscale www.hyperscale.com
Tony Matteliano's Scale Modelling Index
    www.scalemodelindex.com
International Plastic Modelers' Society (USA)
    www.ipmsusa.org
International Plastic Modelers' Society (UK)
    www.ipms.uk.co.uk
Osprey Publishing
    www.ospreypublishing.com

APPENDIX B – SELECT BIBLIOGRAPHY

Archer, RD and Archer, VG *USAAF
    Aircraft Camouflage and Markings 1941-
    1947: The History of Usaaf Aircraft
    Markings, Insignia, Camouflage & Colors,*
    Schiffer Publishing Ltd., Altglen, 1997
Bell, D *Air Force Colors 1926-47* (3 vols),
    Squadron/Signal Publications, Carollton,
    1979, 1980 and 1997
Cross, R and Scarborough, G *P-51
    Mustang – Their history and how to model
    them,* Classic Aircraft No.3, PSL,
    London, 1973
Ethell, J and Bodie, W *War Eagles in Original
    Color,* Widewing, Georgia, 1995
    Pacific War Eagles in Original Color,
    Widewing, Virginia, 1997
Ethell, J and Simonsen, C *The History of
    Aircraft Nose Art,* Motorbooks, Osceola,
    1991
Freeman, RA *The Mighty Eighth,* McDonald,
    London 1970
    The Mighty Eighth War Diary, Jane's,
    London 1981
    The Mighty Eighth War Manual, Jane's,
    London 1984
    The Mighty Eighth in Colour, Arms &
    Armour, London 1991
    The Ninth Air Force in Color, Arms &
    Armour, London 1995
    P-38 – Classic USAAF Colors 2, Classic,
    Crowborough, 2001
    P-47 – Classic USAAF Colors 3, Classic,
    Crowborough, 2002
Hess, WN and Ivie, TG *Fighters of the Mighty
    Eighth 1942-45,* Motorbooks, Osceola,
    1990
Holmes, T *American Eagles Classic USAAF
    Colors 1* Classic, Crowborough, 2001
McDowell, E *P-47 Thunderbolt, European
    Theater,* Squadron/Signal Publications,
    Carollton, 1998
    P-47 Thunderbolt, Pacific Theater,
    Squadron/Signal Publications, Carollton,
    1999

Rust, Kenn C *Air Force Story – 5th, 7th, 8th, 9th, 10th, 12th, 13th, 14th and 15th Air Forces*, Aviation Historical Album, California, 1975-82
The 9th Air Force in World War II, Aero Publishers, California, 1967
Scutts, JC *P-51 Mustang Aces of the Eighth Air Force* (Osprey Aircraft of the Aces series No. 1) Osprey Publishing, Oxford, 1994
P-51 Mustang Aces of the 9th and 15th AAFs & the RAF (Osprey Aircraft of the Aces series No. 7) Osprey Publishing, Oxford, 1995
P-47 Thunderbolt Aces of the Eighth Air Force (Osprey Aircraft of the Aces series No. 24) Osprey Publishing, Oxford, 1998
Stafford, G *Aces of the Eighth*, Squadron/Signal Publications, Carollton, 1973
Stanaway, J *P-38 Lightning Aces of the Pacific and CBI* (Osprey Aircraft of the Aces series No. 14) Osprey Publishing Ltd., Oxford (1997)
Weatherill, D *Aircraft and Aces of the 9th, 12th and 15th Air Forces*, Kookabura, Melbourne, 1978

8TH AIR FORCE

The following 8th Air Force fighter units have had new histories or reprints of earlier ones published in the last three decades or so. Wartime or immediate postwar histories are not included.

4th Fighter Group

Fry, G *The Debden Eagles*, Walker Smith Inc, USA, 1970
Ethell, J and Fry, G *Escort to Berlin*, Arco Publishing, New York, 1980
Hall, Grover C Jr *1,000 Destroyed*, Ace Printing, Texas, 1962

20th Fighter Group

Mackay, R *The 20th Fighter Group*, Squadron/Signal Publications, Carollton, 1995
Ilfrey, J *Happy Jack's Go Buggy*, Schiffer Publishing Ltd., Altglen, 1998

55th Fighter Group

Gray, John M *The 55th Fighter Group versus the Luftwaffe*, Specialty, Minnesota, 1998
Littlefield, Robert M *Double Nickel, Double Trouble*, RM Littlefield, California, 1993

56th Fighter Group

McClaren, D *Beware the Thunderbolt*, Schiffer Publishing Ltd., Altglen, 1994
Freeman, R *56th Fighter Group* (Osprey Aviation Elite series No. 2) Osprey Publishing, Oxford, 2000
Hess, WN *Zemke's Wolfpack*, Motorbooks, Osceola, 1992

78th Fighter Group

Fry, G *Eagles of Duxford*, Phalanx, Minnesota, 1991

339th Fighter Group

Harry, GP *339th Fighter Group*, Turner Publishing, Kentucky, 1991

352d Fighter Group

Powell, Robert H, Jr *The Bluenose Bastards of Bodney*, Taylor, Texas, 1990
Ivie, Thomas G *352d Fighter Group* (Osprey Aviation Elite series No. 8) Osprey Publishing, Oxford, 2002

353d Fighter Group

Rust, K *The Slybird Group*, Aero Publishers, California, 1968
Cross, GE *Jonah's Feet are Dry*, Thunderbolt Publishing, Suffolk, 2001
Price, Bill *Close Calls*, Aviation Usk, Washington, 1992

355th Fighter Group

Marshall BC *Angels, Bulldogs & Dragons*, Champlin Fighter Museum, Arizona, 1984
Wells, K *Steeple Morden Strafers 1943-45*, Egon, Herts, 1994
Wells, K *Wimpeys to Mustangs*, East Anglia Books, Herts, 1999

356th Fighter Group

Miller, Kent D *Escort*, Academy, Indiana, 1985

357th Fighter Group

Olmsted, M *The 357th Over Europe*, Phalanx, Minnesota, 1994
Rust, K *The Yoxford Boys*, Aero Publishers, California, 1971
Roeder, J *The 357th Fighter Group*, Squadron/Signal Publications, Carollton, 2000

359th Fighter Group

Smith, Jack H *359th Fighter Group* (Osprey Aviation Elite series No. 10) Osprey Publishing, Oxford, 2002
Mustangs & Unicorns: A History of the 359th Fighter Group, Pictorial Histories Publishing Co., Montana, 1997
Miller, Kent D *Jigger, Tinplate and Redcross*, Academy, Indiana, 1987

361st Fighter Group
Gotts, S *Little Friends*, Taylor, Texas, 1993
Cora, Paul B *Yellowjackets!*, Schiffer
    Publishing Ltd., Altglen, 2002

364th Fighter Group
Joiner, O W (Ed) *The History of the 364th
    Fighter Group*, Walsworth, Missouri, 1991

479th Fighter Group
No recently published history.

9TH/12TH/15TH AIR FORCES

1st Fighter Group
Mulllins, John D *An Escort of P-38s*, Phalanx,
    Minnesota, 1995

31st Fighter Group
Kucerna, DC *In a Now Forgotten Sky*, Flying
    Machines Press, Connecticut, 1997

79th Fighter Group
Woerpel, D *In a Hostile Sky*, Schiffer
    Publishing Ltd., Altglen, 2001

52d Fighter Group
Burke, LG and Curtis, RC *American Beagle
    Squadron (2nd FS)*, American Beagle
    Squadron Association, Maryland, 1987

82d Fighter Group
Blake, S *Adorimini (Up and At 'Em!)*, 82nd
    Fighter Group History Inc., Idaho, 1992

325th Fighter Group
McDowell, E *Checkertails*, Squadron/Signal
    Publications, Carollton, 1994
Mcdowell with Hess, H *The Checkertail Clan*,
    Aero Publishing, California, 1969

353d Fighter Group
Miller, Kent D *Seven Months over Europe*,
    Miller, Ohio, 1989

354th Fighter Group
(Anon) *History in the Sky*, Taylor, Texas, 1992
Ness, WH *354th Fighter Group* (Osprey
    Aviation Elite series No. 7) Osprey
    Publishing, Oxford, 2002

ACKNOWLEDGMENTS

Many thanks to the following individuals and organizations that helped this project reach fruition: Gaston Bernal, Jr of AeroMaster; Accurate Miniatures; Claudine Chandy of Accountability; Tom Frisque of Aviation Usk; Humbrol Ltd; Kevin Nunn of Brigade Models; Brian Marsh; Binney & Smith (Revell-Monogram); Lynn Sangster of Historex Agents (UK representatives for Verlinden Productions); Thierry Decker for his P-40L profile; Alan Griffith from AMtech; David Klaus and Scott Battistoni from Meteor Productions; Lewis Nace from Testor; Dana Bell; and all the modelers whose kits appear in The Gallery chapter – Chris Wauchop, Darren Mottram, and Mick Evans. Finally, a special thank you to Brett Green.

INDEX